My Internet Horse

Emma White

Illustrations by Jane Hill

authorHOUSE®

AuthorHouse™ UK Ltd.
500 Avebury Boulevard
Central Milton Keynes, MK9 2BE
www.authorhouse.co.uk
Phone: 08001974150

First published by AuthorHouse 11/9/2009

ISBN: 978-1-4490-2883-1 (sc)

This book is printed on acid-free paper.

Having lost my previous much loved HORSE to colic just over ten years ago, I had always thought I would never be able to own another horse again. I was completely heart broken when Solie had to be put to sleep. It came as a complete shock when Solie got colic, as she had never showed any signs of it in the eight years that I had owned her. She was aged approximately 23 years when she died. She was a 15.1hh chestnut mare, but not your typical chestnut mare at all. She was a great all round horse with such a huge personality and I think I had always thought that I would never be able to replace such a loveable friend as Solie. This is why for the past ten years I hadn't even thought about having another horse. My hectic lifestyle as a mum of two young boys, being a full time student nurse in my 2nd year of university and not to mention owning a high maintenance beagle, left me with very little spare time!

Tuesday April 10th 2007 -
The day that was to change
my life completely.

During what should have been a study period at home, I found myself looking at horses for sale on a website which I had stumbled across. After what seemed like just a few minuets of looking at various horses, I saw the horse I knew I had to have. The description of this horse for sale was ***** A True Family Horse****** 15.2hh Black Gelding 8yrs old, Ride and Drive, great with kids, loves cuddles and being groomed. The advert stated that he had hunted, done a bit of show jumping and cross country and had been involved with pony club events. There were three photos of this horse. One was with a little boy, probably no older than about 6 years old sitting on his back in a yard, with no more than a head collar on and no one holding him. The second photo was of the horse standing in a field with two kids on his back, again, with just a head collar on. The final picture was of him harnessed up and standing with his trap behind him with three kids in transit.

He looked absolutely gorgeous and I thought to myself that if he was that great with those kids, he would be that great with my kids. I could then teach my kids to ride and we could have a family horse!! I was so smitten I just had to email the seller to get more information. The advert suggested that the seller lived in the south of the UK in a place I had never heard of. I frantically typed in my email address, stating that I was very interested in this horse for sale and wanted to arrange to view it as soon as possible, I finally left my mobile number.

The following morning, I received a telephone call from a lady who called herself Amanda. She said she was calling about the email I had sent regarding the horse that was for sale. I excitedly asked her where she was as I was very interested in coming to view the horse. She replied, "That may be a little difficult as we live in France." I was absolutely gob smacked!

"Oh," I said. When I mentioned the address in the advert, she waffled on about a relative of hers living in this area, and felt that people may have been put off the horse if she had stated where she really lived. Mind you, she would have been right! "So how am I expected to buy a horse without seeing it?" I asked. She tried to reassure me by saying that a few other people had bought horses over the Internet from her, all of which had worked out wonderfully. She did however, say that if I was unhappy with my purchase I could always send him back and she would try to find me something more suitable. She explained that previous buyers had paid the agreed price into a bank account plus shipping fees of £400.00. The horse would then be vetted and sent on a consignment with other horses coming over to England. Admittedly, this whole scenario really scared me. She stated that she lived in the south of France and that she had her own farm. She went on to say that she had many horses and although she hated parting with any of them, she was just running out of room and so needed to re-home a few of the older ones.

Amanda was an English lady who sounded very knowledgeable and genuine. The thought of parting with money a month or so before my horse turning up freaked me out a bit. I have never been a gambler, nor have I ever had savings to speak of, so it really was a big deal to me. The next question I asked her about him was, "What is he called?"

Looking back, I can remember an awkward silence before she threw out "Jet." At the time I did not think this was at all suspicious. I then asked her how much she wanted for him. She replied "£3000, plus shipping." I found myself asking whether she would accept £2500. She asked me to hold for a minute while she spoke with her husband and when she returned to the line, she said that was fine and that it would be a total cost of £2900 including shipping fees.

"Ok" I said. "I will have a chat with Tom, my hubby, and give you a call back when we have discussed it."

She replied, "Please don't take long deciding, as I won't be able to hold him long for you." Well, I got off the phone feeling like a giddy 12 year old girl. Was this really happening? Could I really be getting a new horse? Then… reality set in. Just how was I going to pay for this horse? I was only a student, and what would Tom say when I told him?

When Tom got in from work that evening, he hadn't even had time to take his shoes off. I said to him, "Quick, come into the office, there's something I want to show you." He studied the photos of Jet on the Internet, and just looked at me smiling. "Yes," he slowly replied, "what's going on?" I excitedly explained everything I knew so far and asked him what he thought. I think Tom had always known deep down that I would have another horse, but this had taken him completely by surprise. Ever-practical Tom, asked how much he was, and then said, "Ok, where are we going to get that kind of money from?"

I said, "We can sell Beau" (the BMW). Some months ago, we had re-mortgaged and kept enough money back so that I could buy my dream car, a BMW. It wasn't brand new, but it was truly a dream come true. We called her Beau. "I'll get a smaller car and with the balance, I can pay for Jet."

He looked quite shocked, as he knew how much I loved my car, but he just said; "It's up to you, if it's really what you want." At that moment, I thought how lucky I was to have Tom. I think his philosophy was, 'anything to keep her happy - within reason!' I found myself jumping around the room. I called the kids into the office to meet their new family friend. They had huge smiles on their faces when I told them all about Jet!

Thursday April 12th 2007 –
Oh my god, what am I doing?

I got out of bed that morning, after not very much sleep. The excitement had almost turned to dread. The giddy 12 year old had turned back into the ever practical person, worrying about finances and the prospect of being a horse owner once again. I sat down with my cup of coffee, looking at a special photo of Solie and me together, and wondered what she might think about it all. I sort of felt as though I was betraying her by thinking about owning another horse. I realise how stupid that sounds, but that's how I felt. I found myself having a few tears. I had never done anything so 'off-the-cuff' as this before. Was I really capable of going through with it?

Later on that day, I felt that before I could even think about pursuing this any further, there were lots of questions I needed to ask Amanda, in order to find out whether or not Jet was suitable for our family. I compiled a whole load of questions that I was going to ask Amanda about Jet. I rang her that evening and said that I was fairly interested but there were some essentials I needed to know prior to commitment. I asked if he came with tack… he didn't. I asked if she had any video footage of him… she didn't. I asked if he was a registered horse with papers… he wasn't. I asked if he had sustained any injuries or illnesses throughout his life… he hadn't. I asked what bit he was ridden in and she said a 'Happy mouth.' I asked if he was freeze-marked or micro-chipped. She said he wasn't, but that he would be micro-chipped with my ownership details prior to departure from France if I were definitely going to have him. I asked what he was like in traffic. She replied, in fairness, that he tended not to see too much traffic as it was very mountainous where they lived. I asked what he was like to be ridden and she explained that he could be ridden every day, or go a month without and still be the same when he was ridden the next time. This sounded very appealing to me; after all, as a busy mum working full time, he may not get exercised every day. The last thing we needed was a hot headed or frisky horse that required riding every day!

Something that I also found quite odd, was that she often referred to Jet as being Friesian, saying things like 'he has typical Friesian traits,' and 'has a fantastic personality,' and that he is 'more of a people horse than a horse, horse,' if you know what I mean. There was however, no mention of Jet being Friesian on the advert, and of course, he didn't have papers!

I got the impression she was trying to get me off the phone quickly. I had bombarded her with all these questions, and I think she felt uncomfortable talking to me. I ended the call by saying, "Thanks for your help, I will go and have a final think and let you know." She reminded me that she needed an answer very soon as she had had many replies from the advert, with a dozen or so people interested in him. After putting the phone down, I felt slightly better about the situation. I got straight back onto the Internet and started looking up Friesian horses. I had only ever heard of Friesian cows before and I was amazed at what I saw. They looked such graceful animals- utterly beautiful. I decided it was now time to start talking to friends about this idea, and get some feedback from them.

I rang by best friend Lindsay who lives 120 miles away and told her all about Jet. Clearly she was as shocked as my family, but equally very happy for me. She did however, have concerns about me parting with such a huge sum of money prior to receiving him. She asked whether it was possible to pay for him on delivery. I admitted that it hadn't even crossed my mind to ask Amanda this, but I would mention it to her next time we spoke. After speaking with Lindsay, I went to see a friend of mine in our village who is also a horse owner; I explained the situation to her. Firstly, she was shocked that I even wanted another horse while I was nearing the end of my course at university, but when I explained everything to her she was horrified! She said, "You don't know these people from Adam. You could end up with a three legged donkey, or even worse, absolutely nothing!!"

I agreed with everything that she was saying, but I answered, "I know all that, but it kind of feels right, I just can't explain it." The only part of the situation that didn't sit right with me was the betrayal that I felt towards Solie. My friend went on to suggest that I seek references from this lady, from people who have purchased other horses from her. I thought this was a great idea.

As soon as I got home, I telephoned Amanda and requested references. She gave me the email addresses of two people who had previously bought horses from her. I told her that once I had had replies from them, I would give her my final decision. The instant I got off the phone, I emailed these strangers, basically saying that I hoped they didn't think I was mad, but I was thinking of buying a horse from Amanda in France who I knew nothing about, and that before parting with my money I wanted to know how they were getting along with the horses that they had purchased from her. Within a couple of hours I had replies from both, stating how wonderful their horses were and how they would never hesitate in getting others from her in the future. This of course, was just what I wanted to hear, and at the time, I never thought how suspicious this was - Amanda giving me these contacts, and within an hour or so I had glowing reports from both! One of the referees said that she had bought a horse for her disabled daughter. She said what a superb animal it was and how the horse had bonded so well with her daughter. The other referee stated that they had had four or five horses from Amanda, all of which had been excellent and how they would never hesitate in buying other horses from her in the future.

Saturday April 14th 2007–
Time for Beau to go!

Having seen these superb references I had all but made up my mind to buy Jet. All I had to do now was to sort the finances out. I had bought Beau from a local garage near my village and it seemed only sensible to take her back there to search for a far cheaper car and trade Beau in. Although this made me feel sad, as I hadn't had Beau for long, I knew it was all in a good cause. My Jet could be my new BMW!!

Tom and I went to the garage in the afternoon. We tried many makes and models of small cars, and the only one I got on well with was a little Renault Megane (Megan). The garage were very happy to have Beau back as a trade in, and when I explained to them why I needed the money, they couldn't believe I wanted to trade in my BMW 3 series for a horse. I had a feeling the guys there thought I was barking mad! Finances were talked about, and it turned out that I would have approximately £3300 left to play with. In my head I was rapidly thinking, 'Was this going to cover horse, transport, saddle etc.?'

Later on that afternoon, still plagued with guilt, I was in our loft looking for one of the children's toys that had been lost. I had only been there a few moments when, out of the blue, I felt something hit me on the shoulder. I looked around to see what had dropped down, to discover the only thing near me was a photograph of Solie. I sat there gazing at her for a few minutes, feeling all choked up again. All of a sudden, this crazy notion came into my head. I jumped out of the loft with a huge sense of relief. I know how mad this may sound, but I took this as a sign from her that I was making the right decision, and that she was trying to tell me to go for it and everything would be ok. I am a great believer that everything happens for a reason, and at that specific moment in time I felt I was meant to have Jet.

Despite my friends and family being clearly against me agreeing to purchase a horse over the Internet and parting with all my cash, I knew what I had to do. I think quietly, Tom probably agreed with friends and family, but also knew how much this meant to me, so he was happy for me to pursue the purchase of my Internet horse. I rang Amanda to tell her that I would be buying Jet and she was over the moon. She explained that I would have to pay the £2500 cash into her bank account and pay the £400 cash shipping fees into the transport company's bank account. Admittedly, I did think this was all a bit dodgy, but also felt that I was going to prove everyone wrong, and end up with my perfect horse. I did however, ask about the possibility of paying for Jet on delivery and she explained that this was simply not an option, stating that funds were needed upfront to pay for vetting and chipping etc. Although this should have worried me, somehow it didn't. I was prepared to take the risk. I was told that Jet would be vetted and micro-chipped to me later on this week, and within two to three weeks, he would arrive. How excited was I?!!!

Tuesday April 17th 2007 –
Parting With My Money

I took Beau for her last drive to the garage. When I arrived, my little Megan was waiting for me along with a bankers draft for the left over money. I collected my new car and happily drove home, feeling very excited about forthcoming events. Having received all the bank details from various parties, it was now up to me to withdraw cash from our bank account and pay it into theirs. I'll never forget standing in the queue in my bank, feeling scared and very worried about withdrawing this money. The lady who served me had seen me on a number of occasions and we knew each other enough to exchange pleasantries but that was all. She cheerily asked me what I was planning on buying, after requesting to withdraw this money. When I told her, she had a worried look on her face, and said, "Are you sure you know what you are doing? You really are taking a risk."

I felt that I didn't really need this from a virtual stranger and wished that I'd never told her. As I left the bank, I said, "When he arrives, I'll bring you in a photo of him." She gave me an odd glance and I just knew what she was thinking.

I walked around town until I found a Barclays Bank. This is where I had been instructed to pay

Amanda's and the transporters cash into their accounts. As I was standing in the long queue, I could feel beads of sweat appear on my forehead while I was waiting. I can remember almost rocking backwards and forwards, trying to build up momentum so I would be ready to leg it out of the door, but there was something telling me to stay exactly where I was. When I eventually arrived at the cash desk, I smiled nervously at the cashier. I said that I would like to pay £2500 cash into one account and £400 into another, but as I was trying to hand the money over to her, I felt myself not wanting to let go. For a second or two we were having a tug-of-war with the money! "Are you quite sure you want to pay this money into these accounts?" she said quite abruptly.

Very weakly, I replied "Yes", and then let go of it. There was no going back now, my money had gone. I can remember saying to myself, 'Would I ever get to meet Jet?'

Wednesday April 18th 2007

– You call that a vetting?

I rang Amanda to explain that I had parted with my money and wondered what would happen next. She sounded harassed and a bit hot and bothered, saying that it was nearly 30 degrees out there. She explained that she had the vet with her at that time vetting all of her next shipment of horses prior to their departure. Suddenly, I thought, 'Does this sound like a lady who has just a few too many horses that she needs to be rid of, or does this sound more like a dodgy business deal going on?' I wasn't too sure what to make of it all.

She said, "The horses are being vetted as we speak. I'm just taking him a cold drink as its thirsty work chasing these horses up the mountain to carry out the vetting!" She then said, "Got to go- will call you later and let you know how he gets on."

When I put the phone down, I thought to myself, 'Did she really just say that; the vet is chasing the horses up the mountain? And that's what they call a vetting?' I was speechless. I just thought, 'Oh my god, what have I let myself in for?'

Monday April 23rd 2007 –
Oh heck, Jet will need somewhere to live!

I woke this morning in yet another panic. I needed to find Jet somewhere to live! The yard that I kept Solie at was perfect, but unfortunately was now 120 miles away from where I now lived. Having never owned a horse whilst being 'Up North', I didn't really know where to start looking. I thought that I could do with having him fairly close to home. The search was on. I got into my car and drove myself to a small livery yard in my village. It had all the basics, but grazing was limited and the stables were small. I can remember thinking a 15.2hh would have difficulties in turning around in those stables. There were no current vacancies anyway. Later on that day I was out with my dogs, when I saw a couple of ladies riding towards me. As soon as they were close enough I stopped and asked them where the best place was to keep horses locally. They went on to say that they owned their own land behind their house and unfortunately didn't have the facility to take on more horses. They then asked me if I had tried the livery yard, which I had already been too. They apologised and said they couldn't think of anywhere else. "Never mind", I said, "Something will turn up," I hoped!

When I got home I remembered an empty field that I had seen when I'd been out walking the dogs. It had got new post and rail fencing around it and was only about half a mile away from home. I bundled the kids into the car and drove over there. The only nightmare was that in order to get to it, you had to cross a railway line with manual gates. The kids thought this idea was great fun, so when we arrived at the gates, we all got out and telephoned through to the signalman telling him we wanted to cross. He said that it was safe to do so and my eldest son opened up both gates for me to drive across then he closed them up behind me. A few moments later we had arrived at the house that appeared to own this piece of land. I made the kids stop in the car, whilst I knocked on the door. After a few short seconds the door opened and a lady in her forties was standing in the doorway, staring at me and looking rather inquisitive. It was very hard not to notice, but this lady had very large breasts! I couldn't help thinking, 'Oh my god, they can't be real!' I was trying to divert my eyes away without being too obvious. I stuttered and said, "Hello, I was just wondering if you were thinking about renting out your field for horses?"

She said, "Yes, I had been thinking about it, and I have had one girl round already wanting the field, but I didn't think she was suitable."

"Oh, right," I said a bit confused, wondering why she didn't think the other person was suitable. I explained about Jet coming over from France in a couple of weeks and that I needed somewhere quite urgently for him.

"If you've got a few minutes to spare," she said, "I'll show you around." We walked around the grounds.

She had two lovely newly built wooden stables and approximately fifteen acres split into various paddocks.

'This would be ideal,' I thought. The owner, Melanie, explained that she did not know anything about horses but felt that her land would look far prettier with horses on it. I had a chuckle to myself, thinking she obviously hadn't ever seen horse's fields in the winter; they wouldn't look very pretty then! Melanie appeared eager to get her little livery business under way and asked me if I wouldn't mind helping her achieve this. 'Well,' I thought, 'I have landed on my feet!!'

When I walked around the fields I noticed a rather large problem. Both paddocks were riddled with ragwort. I explained to her that this would need to be taken up prior to Jet going in there as it is a highly poisonous plant for horses. I said that I would be more than happy to help remove it. We discussed livery costs and she said she would charge me £20 per week, for grazing and stabling, which I felt was reasonable. Feeling very chuffed with myself I said my goodbyes and agreed to go back the following day to start digging up the ragwort. Melanie rallied her kids round to help me dig up the ragwort, without them I don't think I would have managed, there was simply too much of it. Approximately twenty wheelbarrows-full later, it had mostly been dug up and was set aside ready for burning. It nearly killed me pulling it up, but I knew I couldn't have allowed him in the same field as the ragwort, and I just hoped it wouldn't grow back with a vengeance next year.

Thursday April 26th 2007 –
Will he arrive or won't he?

I rang Amanda again. She had promised to call me after the vetting to let me know how Jet had got on and what would happen next. Of course I hadn't heard anything! She apologised for not getting back to me, stating that her life had been rather hectic at the present time. She said all had gone well; he had passed his vetting and had been micro-chipped with my details ready for his journey to England. She hoped that the paperwork would be ready in time for a shipment out of France on the 5th of May. I was filled with excitement. I told Tom and the boys and rang my mum and sister with the news. My mum and sister however, were far less excited. They believed that it was all a scam and that I would never receive my Internet horse.

During the next few days I was backwards and forwards to Melanie's home, digging up the remainder of the ragwort, and generally organising things in preparation for Jet's arrival. Melanie seemed like a really nice lady. She was one of these people who had an air of authority about her. I got the impression that she was quite a materialistic person, who enjoyed talking about her breast enlargements, her expensive 4x4 and her wonderful home that had nearly tripled in price since she moved in a few years back. Although I was extremely grateful that Jet was able to go there, I couldn't help but feel as though Melanie and I may not get on completely.

Friday 4th May came and I still hadn't heard anything from Amanda, so I felt it was necessary to call her again. I could tell that I was getting on her nerves, but if only she had kept me in the picture, I wouldn't have needed to keep ringing her. She explained that Jet's paperwork hadn't been sent back to her and without it he couldn't travel. She hoped that it would arrive early the following week and said that if this were the case he would go at the end of the following week. I told Amanda that I would call her the next Tuesday to see if it had arrived. I was bitterly disappointed, and couldn't help feel that friends and family were just waiting for me to tell them that I'd been had!

Tuesday May 8th 2007 –
Will he arrive or won't he?

As arranged, I called Amanda. Finally Jet's paperwork was back. "Jet just needs to have his second part of the vetting then he'll be ready for transportation in next to no time," she said.

"Hang on a minute Amanda" I fumed, "You told me that he had already passed his vetting!"

She waffled on about Jet having had his individual vetting, but the shipment of horses prior to departure had to go through a group vetting. All this time, I had tried to stay positive, dismissing friends' and families' negative attitudes about the whole thing. After this telephone call I started to believe that it was all going to go horribly wrong. Amanda went on to explain about the transport company that she uses. She told me that the man responsible for delivering the horses to the UK was a man called Clive. She gave me his mobile telephone number and said that Clive would call me when Jet was on board and on his way to England, which should be Saturday 12th May. The transport company mainly carried out international deliveries of horses, and Amanda rated them very highly. Saturday 12th May came. I waited until about tea time and had still heard nothing. I telephoned Clive who said he was currently in Portugal and would be for the next three or four days or more. He went onto say that he hadn't planned on being at Amanda's for at least another week or so. I just wanted to scream!

Monday May 14th 2007 –
Will he arrive or won't he?

S till having heard absolutely nothing from Amanda in France, I decided to call her again; I was now also starting to dread the amount of my next phone bill. She told me that one of the horses on Jet's shipment had failed the final stage of vetting because they had discovered that she was pregnant, and as a result, they had been busy trying to sell another horse so that it could travel in her place. She actually apologised for the delay and said that she had now been able to fill this mare's space and that Jet would be leaving Monday 21st May. I couldn't help but not get excited, as I had now heard this on several occasions.

I think Amanda could sense my dismay, and instead of her usual can't wait to get me off the phone attitude, she was actually quite chatty. While she was in a good mood, I asked her how Jet was. She said he was fine, but getting bored. Apparently once horses have passed vetting stage, they remain in a barn until they travel. So, bless him, he had been cooped up in this barn for over a week already and had another week to go. She promised that Clive would call me as he left her place on Monday 21st May to give me an idea of when Jet would arrive.

Monday May 21ˢᵗ 2007 – Jet's
on his way to England!

It got to about 4pm and still I hadn't heard anything. Amanda had previously given me Clive's telephone number, so I thought I would give him a call. To my surprise, a very chirpy sounding man answered "Hello," he said, "who's this?"

I replied, "Its Emma, I understand you are bringing my horse to England for me?" Clive went on to say that he had eight horses he was bringing to England from Amanda's place. I can remember thinking that he must have a huge lorry if he can fit 8 horses in it! I asked if Jet had loaded ok, and if he was travelling well. He said they all loaded first time and that they all seemed ok.

"As for telling which one is yours," he joked, "at this present moment, it could be a bit tricky, as they are all black and all very similar!"

I had another of those dreaded thoughts in my head, 'Well if he can't tell them apart, how am I going to know if I have got the right horse?' After a few seconds, I thought how ridiculous I was being, and that of course he would know who belonged to whom. At least I hoped he would! He said that once they got to England they would be heading for his yard where the horses would be unloaded, stabled for the night and fed. He expected it to take him at least 24 hours from Amanda's to get to England and then it would be a further 4 or 5 hours getting to his yard from there. He said that Jet should arrive with me, all being well, Wednesday 23rd May at tea time.

For some insane reason, I really didn't think it would take that long. I had concerns over the horse's wellbeing, travelling for so many hours, especially in the heat we were experiencing at that time. Clive reassured me that they would all be fine, that the lorry had air-conditioning for all the horses and very comfortable standings. This made me feel a whole lot better. To hear that Jet was on his way though, and having been given a rough delivery time, I found myself feeling all giddy again. I immediately rang the family and told them. I think they were pleased that Jet was actually on his way, even though they wouldn't believe it until they saw him. In my excitement, I rushed down to our local saddlery and bought almost the entire contents of the shop. My Jet was going to want for nothing!

I had very little sleep that night with all the excitement that this was the day I was finally going to meet my Internet horse. I sat with my coffee looking at the photos of him which were still on the horsey website. I couldn't quite believe that in only a matter of hours, I was going to greet this rather large, handsome chap, and that he really would belong to me. I was floating on air for most of the day. I went down to the yard just to make sure everything was ready for Jet's arrival.

Amanda had already warned me that due to the length of time the horses had been travelling, Jet may be very dehydrated when he arrived, and to offer him water as soon as he got home. Melanie's husband had bought a big plastic water trough, which he had connected to the mains water supply, so I filled his trough ready for him. I did my final walk around the field to make sure there was no leftover ragwort anywhere, and it was all fine. I really was just waiting for my horse now! As I sat waiting for the phone to ring, it crossed my mind that Jet could possibly be very lonely when he got here as there would be no other horses around. My friend Emily had mentioned that she knew a man called Mark at the local riding school that had his horse on full livery there, but he actually lived in the same village as me. I wondered if he might be interested in moving his horse closer to home. I called Emily and asked her to mention this to Mark when she next saw him. Later on in the day, he called me to say that he would be interested, if he was happy with the yard when he came to see it. I gave him Melanie's telephone number so that he could arrange to see the place.

I remained at the yard for some time that afternoon with Tom and the boys, just waiting for the phone to ring. It got to about 6pm and I decided to give Clive another call to find out how close they were. He sounded a bit harassed when he answered the phone and explained that things hadn't gone quite according to plan. 'Oh, here we go I thought!' He said that on his last but one drop-off, there was no owner waiting for him. He had tried to contact the owner, but with no luck, so he had to hang around waiting for him. In view of this, he felt his only option was to organise another transporter to continue Jet's journey home. He said that he had already made the arrangements and that a woman was on her way over to meet him and to collect Jet. I asked with all this going on what time was I likely to be getting him, he said it would now be nearer to 10pm. I can remember thinking, 'My poor horse, he has been travelling since Monday, how much more is he going to be able to take?' I thanked Clive for getting Jet safely to England. He said that he had given the transporter my mobile number so that she could contact me when she got nearer to home, in order to get directions to the yard. When I got off the phone I told the family what was happening. The boys went to bed feeling really fed up that night as they had been so looking forward to meeting our new family friend. I felt utterly exhausted. I sat on the couch feeling as though I could just cry my eyes out. More than anything, I felt very sad for Jet. I can remember saying to myself, that after all this bad luck and let down, it really couldn't get any worse!

At approximately 10pm the phone rang. I nearly fell off the sofa as I jumped up with excitement! It was the transporter whose name was Davina. She explained that she was still over a hundred miles away from us and gave me the choice of either continuing her journey, (in which case Jet would arrive early hours of the morning) or she said she was fairly close to a yard she knew with an empty stable. She suggested that she could off load Jet for the night and set off again early in the morning.

For me there was no choice to make. "No," I said, "please get him off that lorry and give him a break." She agreed and said she should be with us at approximately 9am the next morning. I went to bed feeling quite content that Jet was going to be stabled and fed for the night.

Thursday May 24th 2007 –
Jet's arrival day

I got up early and helped get the kids ready for school. Once again I was filled with excitement. Tom took the boys to school whilst I flew down to the yard. I had arranged to meet my mum there. She was still unconvinced at this point that I was even going to receive my horse. When I arrived at the yard I got to meet Mark. Melanie had shown him around and he decided to move his mare here, as it was going to be far cheaper and much more convenient for him. I was chuffed to bits at the thought of Jet having a friend to share this large field with and hoped that Mark would take her there sooner rather than later!

My mum, Mark and I were chatting and just kicking our heels waiting for the grand arrival of Jet. At about 11am, I called Davina who said that she had been held up in some traffic, but all things being equal she should be with us for about midday. I explained to her that her Sat Nav would direct her to as far as the railway crossing and then tell her that she had reached her destination (which was strictly speaking untrue!). I asked her to call me when she arrived in the village and that I would meet her at the crossing to direct her to the yard.

She agreed. "Won't be long" she said, "He seems like a really nice little pony anyway."

'Little pony!' I thought, 'I hope they have sent me the right horse!' I assumed it must have just been a figure of speech. The excitement was almost too much for me to take!

It got to 12.20pm, and a silence had fallen among us. Seconds later, my mobile phone rang. I nearly dropped it with the shock of it ringing! My heart was pounding so much I thought it was going to leap out of my chest. When I looked at the number calling I knew it was Davina. I hurried to answer the call. I heard a voice say "Hello, I'm just coming in to the village."

I said "Great, I'll drive down to the crossing and meet you there." I looked at my mum with a huge big girly grin on my face, "He's here, he's here!"

"I gathered that!" my mum said. I grabbed for my car keys and told my mum and Mark that I would be back in a few minutes. I ran over to Megan, jumped in and started her up. I drove down to the crossing and reversed into a space and sat waiting for the big plush horse lorry that I was expecting. My heart was going ten to the dozen, but at the same time, I felt as sick as a dog. I decided to get out of the car for some air but as I closed the car door, I saw what looked like a lorry driving towards the crossing.

A little voice in my head was squealing, "It's Jet, he really is here!" I blinked and had a second glance, and yes it was definitely a horse lorry that was coming towards me.

I ran over to the crossing phone and picked it up. It rang a few times before it was answered by the grumpy man I hated speaking to. I explained that a horse lorry was going to be crossing and he told me that we would have to wait for 2 trains to pass first before we could cross. This was like torture! I checked to see that the track was clear and ran through the hand gate, over the railway lines to the horse lorry to explain the hold up to Davina. She wound down the window and said that was fine.

She was nothing like I was expecting. You know when you build a mental image of a person in your mind? She certainly wasn't anything like I had pictured. In fact the lorry was nothing like I had imagined either, it looked a bit rough and tatty. Just then I heard a whinny from the lorry. Well, I could have cried. I felt myself welling up. I just wanted to see him and give him a huge fuss and to show him his new much loved home and family. Finally the two trains crossed and I opened up the gates to allow Davina to drive across. I closed them behind her and then asked her to follow me up the road to the yard. It was only another two minutes drive, and the entire way down the lane I found myself looking in my rear view mirror, looking at this tatty lorry with my Jet in it.

When we arrived at the yard, I pulled Megan up on the verge out of the way. Davina shouted to me from the window, "Where do you want him?" I said that I would open the yard gates for her to reverse into then we could off-load Jet safely. I stood there with my mum watching the lorry backing up towards us. My fists were clenched with the excitement. Suddenly I heard a loud crash, followed by a stumble of hooves! I realised what had happened -she had reversed into Megan! My heart missed a beat, or so it felt. My immediate concern was for Jet. I thought 'I can worry about the car later.'

Davina stopped the lorry and jumped out. "What was that?" she exclaimed.

"You've hit my car!" I replied. "Don't worry about that for the moment though, let's just get Jet out and make sure he is ok." She decided to leave the lorry where it was and proceeded to the back of the lorry to pull the ramp down. I went over to help her.

The ramp came slowly down, and again I heard a little whinny. Jet was right at the back of the lorry, and at this point I still couldn't see him. I was alarmed by the fact there was a big heavy partition lying on the floor very close to his feet, which could have been bumping into him at any stage of the journey. Davina just slid it over to the side of the lorry and then proceeded to open the partitions. After all this wait and worry; there he was, just standing there. I was still outside the lorry at the stage looking up at him. There he stood, this little brownish pony that looked really bedraggled. His long main looked to be tangled from his ears to his withers. He had a dull coat that looked like it was falling out in handfuls. He had no travel boots on so his legs had been left completely unprotected for his entire journey; he had no tail bandage or travel rug on. I was utterly shocked at what I was seeing. I also couldn't help but notice that he no hay and no water in the lorry. Davina walked him to the ramp. My feelings and thoughts at this stage were so immense it is hard to recall everything that was going through my mind at the time. I just wanted him off the bloody lorry to make sure he was unhurt. Davina walked him down the ramp and handed him to me. He was wearing this extremely grotty head collar with an equally grotty rope. The first thing I noticed was that he had a gash on his face about the size of a 50p piece. It was definitely fresh and could have happened just then when she crashed into my car, or it could have happened at some point during transit.

I gave him a good look over and felt myself battling with my emotions. I had been ready to feel an immediate connection and love for this horse, but instead I just felt great pity for him. The ordeal of his journey and crash must have been horrendous and he looked so unkempt and unloved. In fact, he wasn't the horse I had seen in the photographs at all. Instead of being a strapping 15.2hh, I would have guessed at nearer 14.2hh or even less! He looked as though his coat had never seen a brush, and although he had shoes on, they were extremely worn and his feet were very long. It had been a long time since he had seen a blacksmith. My poor, poor Jet.

I remembered how thick set the horse in the photo's had been, and how well toned it was. Jet looked to me like a baby, with absolutely no muscle at all on him and certainly not much fat. There was no way that he was 8 years old. I would have guessed at maybe 5 or 6years! While I had been looking him over, he spent the entire time standing there licking my hand and nudging me. I just felt like crying. I felt so sorry for this poor little chap. He didn't really resemble a Friesian horse either, but at the time I put it down to him being unkempt, and hoped that he would look more like one after a few weeks! As soon as I had checked him all over I walked him into his new paddock and led him over to his water trough. I then took his head collar off and stood with him for a good few minutes while he had a huge drink. He then started tucking into the grass. It seemed as though he felt right at home.

While Jet was eagerly chomping on the grass I went over to Davina to discuss my car. She offered to pay me £50.00 cash there and then for the damage. She told me that her friend had borrowed her horse lorry only last year and had pranged it. Due to this accident, her insurance premium had gone through the roof and she wanted to settle without the insurance companies. I told her that I was unable to accept any money off her at the present time as I had no idea how much damage she had caused to my car and therefore would not have known how much to ask for. I told her that my husband was in the motor trade and may be able to get the work carried out at cost price. She wrote down her address details and mobile phone number and asked me to contact her when I had had a quote for the work, to which I agreed. In all honesty, I really didn't care about my car. Perhaps if it had been my BMW, I would have been far more upset! All I could think about now was my Jet. Davina handed me my paperwork for Jet, which should have contained his passport and vetting papers etc.

After Davina had left, my mum, Mark and I stood around talking about Jet, and looking at his paperwork, trying to decipher what it all meant. I did french at school, but was never any good at it and it was a long time ago. The only part that I could understand was, 'Horse's name.' I can remember looking at his name and thinking, 'How odd, surely Jet in French will be Jet,' but his name according to this paperwork was something weird and wonderful and very difficult to pronounce! Between us, we came to the conclusion that I had either the wrong paperwork, or probably more likely, the wrong horse! There was no micro-chipping paperwork with him and certainly no documents which resembled a passport. The more we looked at the paperwork the more confused we got, and so we decided to call it a day.

As Mark was about to leave he said that he would bring his horse Dee to the yard on Saturday morning. I was thrilled for Jet. Mum and Mark went home, leaving just Jet and me. I left him grazing while I went to the yard to mix him a small feed up. This mainly consisted of carrots and chaff. I can remember Amanda mentioning something about mixes and to avoid them where possible, as they would go straight to his head. When I returned to the field I received a huge whinny from Jet. I felt so privileged to have got such a lovely welcome! I put his feed bucket in the middle of the paddock for him and left him alone to eat.

I walked across to the corner of the field where there was some shade and I sat down and watched him eat his feed. He looked very content. It didn't take him long to finish. I gazed at him, wondering what he would do next. I just sat very still and waited. As soon as he had finished playing with his bucket, he looked around, as though to see where I had gone. He then made his way slowly over to me. When he got close, I remained very still and kept my head down. He sniffed my hair and my face and then he sniffed my trainers and started to chew on my laces. I was overwhelmed at his curiosity in me, but nothing could have prepared me for what happened next. After becoming bored pulling at my laces, he turned away as though to walk away, but instead, he pawed the floor and gracefully lay down very close to me. Still feeling emotionally unstable at this time, I just sat there and cried. I will never forget that moment, it was very special. I stayed with Jet for a couple of hours that afternoon, until it was time to pick the boys up from school.

As I was leaving it occurred to me that Jet hadn't had a poo since his arrival. This was a little concerning as he had been here for over 3 hours now and still hadn't passed anything. I was immediately worried that he may have stress induced colic which could have been caused by his travelling. I decided to leave it for another hour or so before calling the vet about it. I got home with only minutes to spare before needing to collect the boys from school. I decided to ring Amanda quickly. When she answered the phone she sounded very surprised to hear from me. I explained my concerns about perhaps getting the wrong horse as he was smaller than I expected and possibly younger than she had told me. Basically, she was lost for words. She did however, state that there had been eight black horses on the initial shipment that were all of similar temperament, and whichever one I had ended up with I should be happy.

I knew it!! I just bloody knew it! Bloody woman!! I knew at that point that my horse had never been called Jet. It was just a spur of the moment name she had made up when I had first spoken to her. He was just one of probably hundreds of horses she got rid of, rather than having a family business like she had told me, just needing to get rid of some of the older horses to make a bit of space for the younger ones. Despite my fury with her, I just explained that he had arrived, albeit not safely and without harm and that he would spend the rest of his days with me, not that she seemed bothered anyway. After putting the phone down, I felt cross that she had lied to me, but then thought, actually I should consider myself lucky as at least I now had my Jet.

I hurried to school to meet the boys. They both came running out with massive smiles on their faces shouting, "Is Jet here yet?" I think they could tell just by looking at the huge smile on my face that he was. They were both really pleased. I was just so excited about getting the children involved with Jet and the prospect of them even riding him at some stage. We went straight home so the boys could get changed and once again headed off to the yard. Driving down the road, the boys could see Jet in the distance. They became so excited, jumping up and down in their seats and squealing his name, even though we were still some way off. When we arrived, we all piled out of the car. The boys didn't even shut their doors they were so eager! Once again Jet gave us all a lovely welcome with a whinny and started to walk over towards the gate.

Before letting the boys into the field, I explained that Jet was bound to feel a little nervous in his new environment and that they should try and stay calm around him. I just didn't want them to scare him and in turn end up getting hurt. The boys walked into the paddock loaded with carrots and brushes. One stood posting carrots into him, while the other brushed him and generally made a big fuss of him! It was evident that Jet was happy for us to be near his face and shoulders, yet the further backwards towards his bottom we went, the more wary he became. This was one of the little tell tale signs that made me think he was either the wrong horse or the advert I had read about him had all been false. Still, I tried not to worry about it too much, after all this was only his first day with us and I felt that it was only fair to expect him to be a little nervous as he had only just met us.

Tom finished work at 5pm and came straight up to the yard from work. "So", he said. "This is our Internet horse then is it. He's not very big is he?" I explained that he definitely was a lot smaller than the 15.2hh that he had been sold as, but I didn't have a measuring stick to find out exactly how big he was. I looked around the field and noticed there was still no poo. I can remember feeling my heart sink. I was so worried about him. Had he got colic? He looked well though, and was happily eating away showing no signs of colicking. Then it dawned on me that perhaps when he had come to lie next to me, he was complaining of a poorly tummy instead. I could feel myself getting into a state about it, especially as my Solie had died from colic. I rang the vet immediately and told them of Jet's story. She reassured me that if he hadn't had much access to food on his journey, it may be some time before he was able to pass anything. She said that if he hadn't had a poo by 9pm, to call her and she would come out to him. We decided to take boys home to give them their tea as they had started complaining of hunger. On the way home I felt myself go very quiet. 'Oh my god,' I thought to myself, 'the nightmare isn't over yet. What if he has got colic?'

On the way home that night, the boys requested chips from the chippy. This came as a relief as by now I was not in the mood for cooking. When we had got the boys sorted for the evening I raced back down to the stables. It must have been about 7pm by this time. As soon as I looked in the field I noticed there were 3 huge piles of poo! Well, I just felt like dancing round the field I was so happy! I rang the vet to let her know that the panic was over. She sounded pleased and thanked me for letting her know. I made a big fuss of Jet and gave him a kiss good night and headed home. I was exhausted and elated all at the same time. As I left, Jet was still eagerly tucking into his grass and seemed content. Despite me still thinking that I had the wrong horse, or had been completely lied to about the horse that was sold to me, I strangely felt that this was all meant to be. I went to bed soon after the kids that night and set my alarm early so that I could walk the dogs down to the field to check that Jet was ok. That night I had the best sleep ever. I felt like a huge weight had been lifted.

Bright and early the next morning, much to the dog's disgust, we walked down to the yard. One of my dogs is a cocky, naughty Beagle called Bert who doesn't care for horses much, so I did wonder what I was going to do with him when I got him there. Metres away from the field Jet threw his head up in surprise to see us and gave us yet another whinny. Bert started barking at him frantically. Jet just didn't seem phased by this at all! I tied Bert up to the gate whilst I went into the field to give Jet his carrots and check him over. He was fine. In all of Bert's excitement he had somehow managed to touch the electric fencing with his nose and got a shock from it. He yelped and yelped and his tail went between his legs. When I managed to unravel his lead we headed for home and he practically dragged me all the way!

Later on that morning after the kids had got off to school I contacted my insurance company to inform them of the damage that had been done to my car. They advised me to take it in to a recommended garage that would provide them with a quote for the work. A couple of hours later I took it in and was shocked at how much damage had been caused. The estimate came out at just over £800. How bloody pleased was I that I didn't accept her cash offer of £50.00! I telephoned Davina to explain the situation to her. She didn't sound very happy about it and said that she still could not go through her insurance company. She did however; ask if I would allow her to pay in instalments. She offered four monthly instalments of £200. I agreed to this and she said she would get a cheque in the post to me that day for her first instalment.

Later on that evening when I went back to the stables, I thought I would bring Jet in and give him a much needed groom. Before getting him, I hung a large hay net outside his stable door so that he could stand there and eat while having a fuss. I wanted him to associate nice things with being caught and brought in. I went over to him in the field with a carrot and his head collar and caught him with no problem at all. He was however very nervous as I was putting his head collar on. I could constantly see the whites of his eyes while I was touching him around his head and his ears. I led him in and stood him outside his stable where I began to groom him. It dawned on me that there was something I really didn't like about the location of the yard. It was situated very close to a motorway, and the constant road noise was getting on my nerves even after being there only a short time! I thought, 'Poor Jet, how must he feel about it?' To add to our problems, the children that lived in the house at the stables were not from a horsey background, so didn't really know how to behave around horses. Don't get me wrong, the kids were great, but due to them not being horse friendly, I did find it quite hard to relax and Jet seemed constantly on edge when they were around.

Jet stood quietly while I groomed him. On closer inspection of his coat, it was definitely a full summer coat that he had. Despite supposedly being pure black, he was a charcoal brown colour. There was no shine in his coat at all. I also noticed that he had loads of small scabs all over him where he had possibly been kicked or bitten or caught on fencing. The farrier had been arranged to visit on Wednesday 30th May, and as far as I was concerned he couldn't get there soon enough! Jets feet were so long, god only knows how long he had been wearing those shoes for. I gave his hooves a good coat of hoof grease as they were extremely dry and cracked. Then I began to brush his legs and found 2 splints on his offside fore and 1 splint on his nearside fore. I wondered what this poor little horse had been made to do to warrant having such bad legs. It was all a mystery, and what with his nerves seeming to be in tatters, I firmly believed that he had not had the happiest of lives in France. Jet didn't seem too interested in his hay; he just wanted to get back to his field. After much elbow grease, Jet had actually got a shine on his coat! It was amazing how a good groom for an hour had almost transformed him. He looked stunning. I put him back in his field where he happily walked off and started munching on the grass again.

Saturday 26th May 2007 - Dee day

A few months previously I had met a couple of friends called Emily and Jenna at the local riding stables. Coincidently, Emily worked at the same place as my Tom, but none of us had realised that we knew each other until one day when Tom turned up at the riding school with the kids to watch me. When Emily saw him, she asked him what he was doing there. When he replied he had come to watch his wife, we realised the connection and we had a right proper laugh about it! Anyway, I could remember Emily often saying that she would have loved a horse of her own but could only ever dream of it as she could never afford it. This gave me an idea. I thought, 'Why don't I see if Emily would like to come in as a share with me? That way she would have the use of Jet up to three times a week at practically the same cost that she paid for one riding lesson a week. Obviously it would help me financially and also when I'm at work I would know that he would be looked after.'

At this time, Emily was aware that I was getting Jet and she also knew that Dee was due to arrive, but she had no idea of what I was going to ask her. I invited her up to meet Jet and hopefully be there for the arrival of Dee. I did of course wonder whether Jet would ever be suitable for either of us due to his nervousness, but at the back of my mind thought he would overcome his fears after his settling in period, and soon be the perfect horse. Emily met Jet and fell in love with him straight away, as I had done. When I mentioned the share to her, she seemed very excited and said she would speak to her partner about it and let me know. Soon after our chat, we could hear the sound of hooves on tarmac. We saw this beautiful skewbald horse being ridden down the road. Jet's eyes looked as though they were about to pop out of his head! He then came trotting to his gate, nostrils wide and tail up. I knew he was very excited!

Dee seemed to take it all in her stride and did not appear the least bit bothered that she had just come to a new home. Mark dismounted and walked her over to the gateway. Jet looked like he had grown several inches in seconds. He was showing off and just looked so happy with his new field mate! Mark popped her into the field and let her go. The two of them trotted around together for a few minutes, had a sniff of each other and instantly looked like best buddies. Wherever one went, the other followed. It was lovely and quite emotional!

We all stood chatting and watching them for some time, Mark explained that because of his work patterns he doesn't get time to ride often and that if we ever wanted the use of Dee we could take her out with Jet. Things just seemed to be getting better and better. Dee stood at approx 15.1hh and was roughly fourteen years old, a stunning looking mare. Mark had owned her for about eighteen months and had been really pleased with her. Emily & I were very excited about the prospect of riding out with each other. I had a call from Emily later that evening to say that she would love to share Jet with me! I was over the moon because Emily was such a nice person, and I knew that Jet would be cared for very much by her. I just hoped that Jet would turn out to be the kind of horse we would want to ride.

Tuesday 29th May 2007 –
The news that I did not want to hear

It was evening time and I was at home watching the telly when the phone rang. It was quite late, so I wondered who could be calling us at this time. This strange voice asked to speak to me. A man stated that he was calling from DEFRA (Department for Environment, Food and Rural Affairs) and he said he was calling because he understood that I had recently taken shipment of a horse who was delivered by a lady called Davina. He asked me if she had been travelling on her own or if there was anyone with her when she delivered my horse to me. I stated that she had been on her own. When I asked him why he wanted to know, he explained that she had been being caught driving illegally high numbers of ponies in her horse lorry and following a court hearing she had been ordered that if she had wanted to continue transporting horses, she must do it under the direct supervision of another person. The man then went onto say that if I wanted to know the full details of this lady then I should google her name and he left it at that. He also said you may need to be called in as a witness at some stage, just to testify that she had been alone when delivering my horse.

I was shocked and intrigued. I turned my computer on immediately and googled her name as advised. When I read the news article relating to her I felt physically sick. This woman owned a large farm and had several horses of her own. Neighbours had been concerned about the welfare of the horses and had called in the ILPH (The International League for the Protection of Horses). Most of her horses had been rugged up despite it being summer and they were all found to be in an emaciated state. If this wasn't bad enough the worst casualty was a mare in foal, although you would never have known she was practically full term looking at her sad gaunt body. After many failed attempts to get her to her feet it was decided that she should be humanely euthanised there and then due to her horrific condition. The other horses were more fortunate and had been found in time, so were taken away to be nursed back to health. Oh my god, how sick did I feel, knowing that Jet had been in the company of this woman? How could anyone treat their animals in this way? I went over and over it in my head and that night I found that I could barely sleep. What a nightmare!!

Wednesday 30th May 2007 –
Farrier day- Or at least meant to be

The farrier was due to arrive at 11am for both Jet and Dee. Just as I had got them both into the yard I had a phone call from him to say that he was no longer able to make the appointment and that he would need to reschedule for Friday 1st June. I was very disappointed mainly due to the fact that Jet was nearly tripping over his own feet because they were so long! I just told myself that he had waited this long so that two more days wouldn't hurt would it?

Thursday 31ˢᵗ May 2007 –
Saddle fitting day

When Jet arrived in the UK all he came with was a scabby head collar, which soon went into the bin. As he came with no saddle or bridle I had made arrangements for a local master saddler to come out and fit Jet for a Wintec saddle. I had also contacted a friend called Sally and asked her if she would come down to the yard with me as I knew the saddler would want to see me on Jet once he had sorted a saddle out for him. I felt that it would be wise to have someone hold onto Jet whilst I got on him for the first time, just to air on the side of caution. After all, for all I knew this could have been a first for him. Sally agreed to help me and turned up at the arranged time. I had now had Jet for a few days and he did seem a little more at ease with me, but when he met these strangers for the first time, I saw the whites of his eyes again and it was obvious he was quite nervous once more.

When a saddle had been chosen for him he asked me to pop on so he could see what it was like once I was on board. I was excited but at the same time I can remember having butterflies about the prospect. Sally had a lunge line attached to his bridle and I mounted as quietly as I could. Jet's ears went back and you could tell he was not entirely comfortable with the situation. Sally walked around and Jet followed. The saddle appeared to fit just fine. Moments later I jumped off and gave Jet a huge hug. I was so pleased with him, and even more excited abut the future rides and adventures that we were going to have together! As soon as Sally and the saddler left, I texted Emily and gave her the good news. She too was really pleased.

When I got home that evening I realised that a whole week had gone by and I had not received a cheque from Davina. I called her, she explained that she had been waiting for a friend of hers to pay her money owed and until she had received that, she couldn't afford to pay me. Normally I would have been more understanding about such matters and given her more time to pay, but considering what I had just discovered about her, I told her that I would take this up with my insurance company and ask them to pay me directly from her insurers (presuming of course she was insured!). The next morning I contacted my insurers who were fantastic. They arranged for my car to be repaired immediately and although it took quite a long time, they did eventually get paid from her insurers.

Friday 1st June 2007 –
First ride out and Farrier day

The farrier was due at 4.30pm today. Mark and I had arranged to ride out together -just down the lane and round the village, so that we could be back in time for the farrier. I felt really nervous again when I first got on Jet, but we just had a walk and they were both very well behaved. When we approached the bottom of the lane, we had to cross the railway line. Luckily for me on our first trip out, there were no signs of any trains. We jumped off at the signal box and telephoned the controller to check that no trains were coming. We were given the all clear and asked to call them back once we had got across safely and when the gates were closed behind us. We did so.

Once back on the horses we went for a quiet walk around the village. While we were walking down the road I had a big grin on my face. I couldn't actually believe that this was really happening! I leant forward to give Jet a gentle pat on his neck for being such a good boy. Just then he suddenly leapt at least three feet in the air and off all four feet! For me this was a very sad moment, he obviously wasn't used to being patted whilst being ridden. Within moments he had soon relaxed and we headed back to the yard. When we got back, the farrier was there waiting for us. He didn't seem happy, firstly because he had had to wait, despite him arriving early for our appointment, and secondly because he had had to get over the railway line, which meant having to get out of his car and manually, do the gates. He made his feelings perfectly clear that he found it a real faff to get across the railway lines!

Before he started shoeing Jet, I explained to him just how nervous he was, especially around men it seemed. Jet behaved remarkably well even though he looked so nervous. The farrier did shout at him once for moving which did not go down well with him or me! Once the job was done I was really pleased. Dee was also very good at having her shoes on. We booked in for another 7 weeks. I text Emily to let her know what Jet had been up to. She was delighted that he had been good for the farrier and was surprised at how well behaved he had been on his first ride out.

I had arranged a ride with Mark and another friend of mine Sienna who lived close to us at 3pm. We met Sienna down the lane and set off down through the fields. Sienna's mare is lovely and Jet seemed only too pleased to be escorted out with two lady friends. The fields and tracks we had ridden on led to a busy road through another village. There was a whole manor of things to deal with whilst riding out on the road; more railway lines to cross, caravans coming past, a bus and smallish motorbikes. Jet took all of these in his stride and remained relatively calm. He carried on plodding down the road with his friends. Isn't it always the bloody way though? I had just been having a discussion with Sienna, saying how lucky I was to find such a good horse, when coming towards us was yet another motor bike. I remained calm and carried on chatting as Jet had already had motorbikes come past him and he had been fine. This however was a different kind of bike. It was the kind with really high handle bars and an extremely loud engine. It sounded like it was back firing as it came past!

Well, I'm not sure if Jet thought he had been shot at, but before I had any clue that this had upset him, we found ourselves bolting down the middle of the main road, narrowly missing oncoming traffic! Ten to fifteen seconds later he came to an abrupt stop at the bollards in the centre of the road and quickly spun round to see where his friends were. I felt sick. 'Oh my god, how lucky we were to be alive?' I thought. I had tried stopping him sooner, but my hands had literally become wrapped and tied in his long mane. Both Mark and Sienna were gob smacked at what they had just witnessed but glad that we were both ok. I could tell that Jet had also been really shaken up, we both stood there trembling.

"I don't think he likes bikes," I said sheepishly. We got home safely and I decided on the way home that it was probably best not to tell Emily in great detail about the incident, just that we had discovered he didn't like this type of motor bike. I didn't want it to put her off completely before she had even started!

Over the next couple of weeks, I met Emily down there on several evenings, we rode just round the village and would take it in turns riding Jet and Dee, Jet even became desensitised to the trains and just stood at the railway gates while they were thrashing past us. With most things he was just so good he really surprised us. I had also contacted our friend Jenna who also used to ride at the riding school and she met us down there on a few occasions and joined us for a walk out some evenings. Fun was had by all. It was unfortunate though, because as it stated in his advert that he was a true family horse, in the ridden aspect he was sadly far from it. I would certainly not have been prepared to put either of my children on him for their own safety. They didn't seem to upset with this, as they just loved coming down to give him carrots and to spend time brushing him.

Wednesday 20th June 2009 –
My poor friend, What a painful fall!

One of my sons friends mum in the village, called Lizzy, mentioned that she would love to come and see Jet. She is a very experienced rider that rides horses on a regular basis and hunts quite frequently. I explained that I would be riding that evening if she wanted to come and see him. When she saw Jet for the first time she thought he looked really cute but was quite surprised at how small he was, as she knew that he was meant to be 15.2hh; she also couldn't believe how young and immature he looked. She helped me brush and tack him up and decided that she would come out for a walk with me while I rode. Jet behaved really well on the ride, and after twenty minutes or so Lizzy decided that she would pop on Jet and ride him back home. He was a really good boy for her to. We had been out for about forty minutes in total and during this time we had been discussing his progress. I told Lizzy that I hadn't even cantered him yet as I felt a little nervous doing so. When we got back to the yard there was an open grass field to the left of us. Lizzy volunteered to pop him in there for a little canter to see what his reaction would be.

She trotted away from me then popped him into canter however as soon as he got into his canter stride he took off sideways down the field at a rapid rate! All I could see was Lizzy heading toward the busy road. My hands went over my eyes for a split second. When I took them away I saw Lizzy lying on the floor with Jet eating the grass nearby. I ran over to her. It seems that Jet did a sudden turn with her to stop himself from going onto the road and she went flying out of the side door! She landed awkwardly on her shoulder and was in quite a lot of pain. I felt absolutely terrible. I helped her up and took her home. She insisted that she was ok, but I knew she wasn't really. I asked her to text me the next day to let me know how she was.

I hadn't heard anything from her by lunchtime the next day so I sent her a text to get an update. I didn't get a reply for some time. When she did finally reply she said that she had had to go to A & E the previous evening where they had confirmed that she had severe bruising to her shoulder. They gave her a sling and advised her to keep her arm elevated for a week or so. She said that she was still in terrible pain and had to take very strong pain killers for a number of days. I felt just awful about the whole situation, especially as she had to have time off work but there was nothing I could do. What had made Jet take off like that? I really didn't understand it. I couldn't help but think I was going to have problems now with Jet, and what made matters worse was that we had no schooling facilities available. We really could have done with the use of a school. The big question going through my mind at this time was, 'Will I ever be able to canter Jet, and if so, will it be safely without him chucking me off too?'

Monday 25th June 2007 –
The great floods of 2007

Over a couple of weeks or so we had some terrific downpours. It wasn't your typical June at all. Bit by bit the horse's field had slowly started to fill with water and it was becoming a real concern. The field was situated approximately 1 mile away from the sea and was at high risk of flooding. There were many ditches in the area, which were there to help with drainage, but unfortunately due to the vast amount of rainfall we had had, the ditches kept filling and the fields kept flooding. I went down to the yard about 6pm that night and as soon as I arrived Jet and Dee whinnied at me. They looked very pleased to see me but I noticed that they weren't making their way over to me. Just then I realised that they had been stranded on top of a small mound in the field and water had come in all around them! I raced to grab their head collars and went running over to them. They were both reluctant to come in and seemed very uneasy wading through the water back to the yard. Eventually I managed to get them into their stables. I telephoned Mark and told him that the horses were going to have to stay in for the night as the field was so bad.

As I got them bedded down for the night and the hay ready for them in their stables I realised that we were going to have a bigger problem on our hands. The water level in the yard was steadily increasing and moving towards the stables. I went home shortly after and told Tom about our potential problem. He said that the best thing to do was to take it in turns doing hourly vigils. I also rang my friend Sally who had her horses in a nearby village and owned a trailer. I thought I should get some emergency plan put into place in case we had to be evacuated. Sally also gave me a number for Greg who owned Eastdale, the livery yard where she kept her two horses and stated that if the need arose she would be more than happy to transport the horses out for us. I telephoned Greg who said that he could gladly accommodate our two horses on a temporary basis as long as they didn't mind sharing a field. I thanked him and said I would contact him the following day to let him know what was happening with us.

That night was simply awful. I can remember Tom getting back from the 1am check. He said that although the horse's stables were still dry at that time, the water was only feet away from the stable doors. The two neighbours just a few hundred yards away hadn't been so fortunate. They had been pumping the water out of their houses for the past hour or so as they'd both had approximately six inches of water inside. I immediately text my friend Sally who said she would be over at 9.30am the next morning to take them to Eastdale. By 7am that morning, the stables were under water; luckily we had got the horses out of their stables before that happened. Walking them out of the yard was no easy task either. My wellies had proven useless as the water level was higher than that of my boots, it was actually higher than the horses knees. Both Jet and Dee seemed very nervous wading through the water, but did it anyway, almost as though they knew that what we were doing was for their own good. We walked them up to the road where we could all dry out, and gave them some hay to munch on, keeping them amused whilst waiting for our lift to arrive.

Tuesday 26ᵗʰ June 2009 –
The first move to Eastdale

Both Mark and I had absolutely no idea how our horses would load into a trailer, we just hoped that they would be good! Sally arrived at 09.30 on the dot and by this time we had booted Jet and Dee up ready for their journey. They both still seemed very relaxed at this time despite all the upheaval and worry of the previous night. Sally got us organised quickly. She got straight out of her vehicle and got the ramp of the trailer down within seconds. I walked Jet immediately up to the ramp where he stopped to have a look inside, and as soon as I put a carrot in front of his nose he walked straight into the trailer and stood like a gentleman! Dee also had a stop and a look, but as soon as she realised that Jet was in there and appeared to be fine, she followed suit. We threw everything into the back of the car and explained to Melanie that we would be back in a week or so, or however long it would take for the water to subside. She didn't seem happy about it, but I hoped that she would understand the need for us to move temporarily.

We followed the trailer to Eastdale; it only took about fifteen minutes to get there. Sally showed us the field that they were going into. It was approximately one acre. The field was in a very rural picturesque location, having a church on one side of the field and pretty looking longhaired cows in the field opposite. The only thing that concerned me was the length of the grass in their field, but I had to remind myself that grass was probably the least of my worries at that time. 'Oh well,' I thought, 'being fat for a week has to be better than needing armbands!' As Jet had been getting regular rides out, his weight was quite good so I just hoped it wouldn't take too long to get it off again once we moved back. We unloaded the horses and put them straight into their new field. They didn't even bother having a look around. As soon as they got in it was just heads down to scoff! They seemed happy, and so were we. It was a big relief knowing that we had got them away from their flooded field. However, it soon dawned on me that as this flooding had happened there now, who was to say it wouldn't happen again there in the future?

Later on that evening we walked the horses up to the yard and decided to have a walk around the block. After being in the yard for a few moments I said to Mark, "Have you noticed anything different about Jet?"

He looked at him and said "What?"

You would not have believed it was the same horse. He was no longer the horse showing the white's of his eyes and appearing fretful most of the time. He just seemed so chilled out it was lovely, and it was the first time that I had seen him like this. I also mentioned to Mark that being there in the countryside the only audible sounds were other horses and birds. There was no flaming motorway sound that meant you had to shout a conversation to someone to get heard! It was so peaceful, it was lovely. One of the best advantages of going to this yard was that it had an outdoor ménage. We decided at some point during the week we should use it.

We went for a stroll around the village that evening and rode off into some nearby woods and back. It was the best ride I had ever had on Jet. It really made us think. What on earth were we doing keeping our horses close to home when Eastdale was only a few extra miles away? There was nothing to offer them in our village at all. The only bridleway was a long way from the yard and it involved walking down a main road to get to it, so we avoided it at all costs. This meant that we were so limited to where we could ride and compared to the rides we had been finding in Eastdale, it made the our village look so damned boring! During that next week, we had discovered other fantastic rides and also made good use of the ménage. I spoke to Mark and asked him whether if there were any places available he would be interested in moving Dee there on a permanent basis. He agreed that it had far more to offer than our previous yard. We spoke to Greg at the end of the week and unfortunately there were no places available at that time. He did however agree to ring us as soon as there were some places. So, the following Monday I popped to our yard to check out the flooding and the water had almost all drained away. I was bitterly disappointed. Transportation was arranged with Sally to take them back to our village the very next day.

As before, the horses loaded beautifully. As we were driving away I couldn't help but feel sad, we had had such a fantastic week. We arrived back at our yard and put the horses back into their field. I wondered at that point what was going through their minds. I wondered 'Were they glad to be back or not?' Melanie came out to meet us and asked us if we wanted a coffee. We said yes and ended up staying there for quite a while. Loyalty and guilt were the only reasons we had gone back. After all, Melanie had set this place up almost for us, so I would have felt bad not going back. Although I knew deep down it was one of the worst decisions I had made, sadly, there was no other choice at that time.

I had just come off a night shift having only had approximately 2 hours sleep, in order to get to the yard for 12pm for the farrier. It was a warm day with a bit of drizzle about. Very wearily I got the horses in and waited for the farrier to arrive. An hour or so had gone by, and although I knew that he could sometimes be a bit late, I thought this was taking it to the extreme, especially as he had my number and could have contacted me! I sent him a text message asking if he was on his way. Five or ten minutes later, he replied saying he was sat at home waiting for a delivery to turn up. After reading this I could feel steam coming out of my ears. I text him back saying, 'Gather your not coming then?'

'No,' he said. I was absolutely furious. I just knew he wouldn't show up, as he had done nothing but complain about getting over the railway lines. Really it should have come as no shock, but to just not turn up, especially when I had dragged myself there whilst been sleep deprived. Arghhhhhhhh! I just wanted to scream. I turned the horses back out and telephoned Sienna who uses a different farrier. I got his details from her and rang him straight away. He sounded lovely, his name was Adam and he agreed to come out and shoe our two horses the following Wednesday. He didn't give me a time, he said he always works out his workload and route the night before, and then contacts his customers with an approximate time. So, the night before as promised I had a text from Adam saying he would be there at about 2pm. The following Wednesday I was down at the yard in plenty of time. I got the horses in, and just before 2pm I saw a van pull up. It was Adam the farrier. I can remember having a smile on my face, a farrier that turns up on time- what a rarity!!

Adam seemed lovely. I warned him of Jet's nervous disposition so he remained very quiet and calm with him and in return Jet was relatively laid back. Whilst I was holding the horses for Adam, I could see a very black sky approaching and within moments rumbles of thunder could be heard in the distance. I warned Adam that if the storm should get close I was likely to make a run for it, as I was terrified of thunder and lightning! I could see the lightning in the sky but it seemed a very long way away, possibly out at sea. I was still very nervous and could feel myself shaking a bit, but Adam was very good and even offered to hold the horses and shoe them at the same time, bless him. I managed to see it through and get the horses back into their field before the heavens opened once again. I booked in for another seven weeks time with Adam and thanked him for doing a very good job. I was so pleased that he was happy to continue looking after their feet, as many farrier's have too many customers and often want to deplete customer numbers instead of increase them.

Tuesday 7th August 2007 –
It was only a matter of time - My fall

It was a lovely day for a ride so I had arranged to meet Emily up the yard for a quiet hack out. Emily was due to ride Dee and I was going to ride Jet. I arrived up the yard at approximately 5pm where I waited for Emily. When she arrived we fetched the horses in together and got them groomed and looking very smart. We tacked them up and shortly after we were ready for our ride. In order to mount, we always had to walk the horses through two gates, which led onto a quiet lane, and on the side of the lane was a large square stone, which we used as a mounting block. I led Jet over first to get on. I stood on the stone and placed my left foot in the stirrup. As I was in the midst of throwing my right leg over to get on, Jet decided to walk off. For a split second I can remember thinking, 'Blimey, do I jump down or do I continue throwing my leg over?' I decided to continue trying to get on but as I threw my leg over his back, I caught my foot on his bum. With the shock of this, he bolted! According to Emily, at this point I did a somersault in the air and landed head first on the road. Jet got over his scary moment very quickly and ran to the nearest bit of grass! To this day I still don't know if I was knocked out or not, but I suspect that I may have been.

I can remember Emily saying, "Oh my god, we need to get Melanie and we need to call an ambulance!"

I kept saying, "No, I will be fine." Despite being in agony, the only think I kept thinking about was, 'If I don't get back on this horse now, I know I never will.' I got up off the floor and said, "Come on, let's just go out a little way." Emily thought that I had completely lost the plot. When I went to get on Jet for the second time, I asked Emily if she would hold him whilst I got back on. She did, and it was easy to see this experience had unnerved him as you could clearly see the whites of his eyes again. Despite this he stood like an angel while I climbed on board. Although I hurt everywhere, I knew just how important this ride was going to be. Emily got on Dee and we wandered off down the road. I don't remember too much about the ride when I look back now and Emily says how worried she was about me. Apparently I kept saying to her, "God, I don't remember what happened, what happened?" Then Emily would tell me. Then, no more than five minutes later, I would repeat the same thing; "I don't remember what happened, what happened?"

Twenty minutes or so into our ride, we met up with some people we knew who also had horses. We were having a chat with them when all of a sudden I realised that I had a terrible headache. I asked Emily if we could set off home as I was also starting to feel a bit sick. As we turned round I felt that my right sleeve was all wet. I rolled it up and noticed blood trickling down my arm. We carried on heading for home. As we approached the last house before the yard there was a huge pile of wood dumped on the driveway. I can remember saying to Emily, "Oh, someone has left all that wood there in the time that we've been out, be careful just in case they have a spook at it." Emily didn't say anything at the time but it was some days later when she told me that the wood had been there on the way out and yes, both horses had jumped at it as they had walked past it the first time they saw it! We got back to the yard, untacked, fed and turned the horses out. I had biked to the yard that night so Emily offered to take me home. I rang Tom and explained to him that I had had this fall and asked him if he could he start running me a bath.

When I arrived home my bath was ready. I got straight into it, although it was very painful when getting in initially. I had many scuffs and scrapes all over my body where I had possibly been dragged on the road. Within moments Tom came into the bathroom, took one look at my battered body and said, "Come on, I'm taking you to A & E". I found it very difficult getting out of the bath as my back was absolutely killing me. Tom had to help ease me out gently. I got dressed with some assistance and it seemed to take for ever. Tom telephoned my mum to explain what had happened and she promptly came over to our house to look after the children while we went to the hospital. When we arrived they asked for a brief history of what had happened. I explained to the best of my ability, bearing in mind I had got a head injury and told them that I had taken the brunt of my fall on my head and back when I landed on the road. They asked me to wait in a holding area. Tom stayed with me and we seemed to be in there for hours. My pain was becoming increasingly worse.

Approximately three and a half hours later a Doctor came to see me. He looked at my notes and asked the nurse why I hadn't been placed on a spinal board. She looked clueless and asked him if I should be put on one at that time. He agreed. I was then taken round to the x-ray department where I had another wait. While I was waiting for my x-rays, a fellow student nurse friend of mine (who had been working on A & E) saw me. Apparently, she stayed with me for about fifteen minutes or so talking to me and asking what had happened. I only found this out however about 3 months after the event because I bumped into her at university. She had said that I was looking much better after my fall, so I asked how she had known about it. That's when she explained that she had seen me that night and had been talking to me for quite some time. I was quite freaked out that I couldn't remember even seeing her!!

Anyway, I had my x-rays and was told no real damage had been done and that I could go home with some pain killers. I was in so much pain at this time I wondered if the x-rays could have been incorrectly read. I could barely move a muscle without searing pain everywhere. I asked who had look at my x-rays, when I was told I couldn't believe my luck. It was a doctor who only the week before I had heard had been trying to resuscitate a conscious patient! I had little faith. For at least 2 weeks I was drugged up to the eyeballs. It hurt to breath, move and sleep. Emily and Tom were really good looking after Jet for me while I was laid up. Emily exercised him while Tom and the kid's poo picked the field on a daily basis for me. Despite the pain, and despite the accident, I was still so pleased that I had got back on Jet to finish my ride. I just kept focusing on how well he had behaved with me following my fall and although feeling a tiny bit apprehensive I couldn't wait to get back on him.

Monday 13th August 2007 –
Handing in my notice

I went up the stables that evening full of dread as I knew I would be handing in my notice. I just had this feeling that it wasn't going to go down well with Melanie, but by the same token I felt that I had to be a little selfish, as I had to think of what was best for Jet, Emily and me now. Whilst being in Eastdale it was clear from the moment we arrived that our village yard was just so wrong for us. Best of all, Jet seemed to love it at Eastdale. Greg had contacted us to tell us about two places that had just become available, so we jumped at the chance. When I arrived at the yard it wasn't long before Melanie came out and asked me if I wanted a coffee. While we sat down with our drinks having a chat, I found an appropriate gap in our conversation. I blurted out that I would be leaving on 3rd September and gave her my reasons why.

Melanie went very quiet on me. I don't think she was expecting me to come out with such a bombshell. I explained my predicament about having such a young and inexperienced horse that was going to need regular schooling etc. She said she understood, but I couldn't help feel that all she wanted to do was give me a slap! She asked me if Mark would be leaving also. I told her that she would need to speak to him about that, although of course I knew he was. I didn't feel it my place to discuss it with her. Over the next few days I saw very little of Melanie. I got the feeling she was avoiding me, although I was actually very glad of this as I knew any contact with her would be awkward. I was still in a lot of pain from my accident at this point so I still wasn't riding. Jet really could have done with being lunged on a regular basis, but due to our location it was just impossible. Roll on moving day!

Wednesday 15th August 2009 –
Jet and the Vet.

Before Jet had even arrived in the UK, I knew that he had never been vaccinated for tetanus and flu, as Amanda had told me that she didn't believe in vaccinating her horses – what a surprise! I had arranged for the vet to come out to start his course of injections and I had also requested that they bring their micro-chipping scanner with them so that I could check owner details with them. This really was the only way I was going to establish if he had initially been meant for me as he should have been scanned with my ownership details. When the vet arrived she came over to make a fuss of Jet and we had a general chat about him and his health. She asked me what he was like whilst having injections. I explained that I didn't know as I hadn't owned him long. She had bought along with her a student vet, so I asked them if they wouldn't mind holding him between them while giving him his jab as I was still in agony from my fall. I felt as though I had broken numerous ribs and I thought, 'If Jet flies up in the air with me, I could be in serious trouble!' Although they agreed, it sounded like a reluctant yes. Luckily for all involved, Jet was a true gentleman for the vet and her assistant.

As they were about to leave I reminded them that I wanted him scanning. She nipped over to her car to get the scanner and she let Jet have a sniff of it before waving it up and down both sides of his neck.

"I hate to tell you" she said, "He isn't chipped."

"How can that be?" I said, "How would he have been able to come into this country without a microchip?" I could tell the vet was as confused as me.

"I have no idea," she replied. "Shall I do him while I'm here?" she asked. So of course I agreed. For this procedure I was very grateful that I wasn't holding onto Jet. It was a sizeable needle that was buried deep in the neck so that the microchip could be released. Poor Jet, he went bonkers! The poor vets had to hold onto him and were dragged around the yard several times. Soon after their departure, Jet calmed down. I made a fuss of him and put him back in his field with Dee. I was in two minds whether to ring Amanda and ask her what on earth had been going on with him, but I then thought, 'Just what is the point?' She probably wouldn't even accept my call, and if she did, I knew she would blatantly lie about it anyway.

Later on that afternoon I had an appointment with my osteopath. I'm not sure why I booked the appointment really but I thought it would help with my aches and pains. When I stripped down to vest top and shorts he said, "Bloody hell girl, looks like you've been hit by a bus!" I told him that I felt like I had been hit by a bus. Unfortunately there was little he could do with me. He just advised me to keep taking the anti- inflammatory pills and pain killers and rest up as much as possible.

I went off down to the yard early as Jet's dentist appointment was for 9am. I got him in and we patiently waited for the dentist to arrive. He seemed like a nice man and asked me if Jet had been having any trouble with his teeth. I explained that I hadn't had him long and that I was trying to get all the routine jobs out of the way. I told him to be very careful as Jet didn't like strangers and it had become more apparent that he really didn't like men! He came into the stable with us and slowly made his way over to Jet. Jet backed off and snorted at him. Luckily the dentist didn't force himself on him; he just took his time with him and spoke very softly to him. You could tell that Jet was very uncomfortable about the whole thing, but he was being really brave and standing very still. The look in his eyes said it all. Once the dentist had completed his examination he said that Jet's teeth had possibly never seen a rasp before and they were in really bad shape, but more concerning Jet had a wolf tooth that needed to be removed. He also said that Jet would need sedating before this procedure could happen.

'Why is there nothing simple?' I thought!! As the vet was due to come out again soon for the second part of Jet's flu/tetanus injection it, seemed only sensible to get the whole lot done at the same time. Poor Jet, I bet he wondered what on earth he had got himself involved with, landing up in some strange cold country with people he didn't understand, people that poked him and jabbed him, and people that kicked him up the bum while getting on scaring him half to death! It must have been quite an ordeal for him.

Monday 3rd September 2007 – The best decision so far - the move to Eastdale – or was it?

We had arranged for Sally yet again to come and collect the horses. We were grateful to her for being so kind. Emily and I had got up to the yard early that morning to try and get everything packed up. I couldn't believe after only a few months the amount of stuff I had accumulated! Tom had managed to borrow a works van, which was just as well as it was loaded from ceiling to floor with horsey stuff. We got the horses in and booted up. They didn't seem to be bothered by all the goings-on so I wasn't sure if they sensed a change or not. I had this feeling that Melanie was going to stay inside while we left. She had made no attempt to come out, but just as Sally arrived she came out with a coffee and a cigarette in her hand. She watched as we loaded the horses and then as we were about to leave I said thanks for everything and told her that I would stay in touch (knowing full well I probably wouldn't). We got into the car and followed Sally down the road. I was so excited I could hardly contain myself!

I just so hoped that Jet and Dee were going to be happy in their new homes. The only problem that I could see at this time was that Jet and Dee were due to be separated when they got to Eastdale; they had strict mare and gelding fields. I kind of wished that they could have just gone back into the field that they had stayed in back in June, but was told that that field was a temporary measure only as it gets used by other people throughout the year. This was a real shame as they did seem to have a close bond. It was obvious that Jet loved Dee far more than Dee loved Jet, but it didn't matter, they just got on well. In the mare field there were only two other girls but in the gelding field there were at least seven boys, all of whom were much bigger than Jet!

I had asked the children to video Jet and Dee's journey up to Eastdale from our car. When we watched this back it was very good footage and they both seemed to travel very well in the trailer. The video kept rolling as we arrived at the stables. We off-loaded the horses and removed their boots and tail bandages. We decided that it would be a good idea to turn one out at a time so we could video them going into their individual fields with their new friends. Dee went out first and in the meantime Jet stood in his stable next to Sally's horse Chunky, in the hope that they would make friends before the big turn out. We followed Mark and Dee up to the field and watched with excitement as he turned her out into the mare field. Dee and the other two mares had a good gallop around followed by much squealing but it wasn't long before they all grazed quite contently with each other.

Now for Jets turn. I could feel my stomach doing somersaults! I was really nervous for him especially as he had some very large horses to contend with. As we walked him down the track towards his field with Chunky, Jet's pace got quicker and his head higher. I think he too was excited about his new home. Dee's field was only two fields away and all of the fields were just separated with electric wire, so although he would be in with the boys he could still see Dee. The other horses could see that a newcomer was on the way and came trotting down the field to meet him at the gate. We had a bit of a fight on our hands trying to push past all these big horses in order to get Jet and Chunky into the field. It was quite daunting really. As soon as I was able, I took his head collar off and got out of the field quickly.

We all stood in safety behind the gate watching. The horses seemed none-too-happy about Jet encroaching on their territory and began chasing him up and down the field. At first I thought this was only natural, as they would need to let him know his place in the pecking order. He had the occasional sniff of a horse, but each horse in turn tried booting him or chasing him around the field. This went on for some time; they didn't allow him to eat or drink for ages. When one horse got tired of chasing him another took over. Even Chunky had a turn. The most upsetting thing of all was to see Jet galloping up and down the fence line calling to Dee and looking to her for comfort, but she was not the slightest bit bothered, after all she had her new girl friends now! I could tell that he was really upset. I stood there with tears in my eyes and couldn't help but think, 'God, what have I done to him?' Dee grazed quite happily with her friends and was completely oblivious to what Jet was going through.

I stayed at the stables most of the day and kept going into see Jet to give him a treat. Each time I would yell or chase any horse that came anywhere near him, but I felt that this was one battle he had to deal with himself. I was on annual leave for two weeks and I spent most of the time at the stables. Poor Jet did not get much let up. It was a simple fact, he was hated by all. I realised that most horses take a while settling into an established herd, but no-one was inviting Jet in at all. He was clearly an outsider, and that was where he was staying.

Monday 10th September –
Wolf tooth being removed- or will it be?

I had arranged for the vet to come out to sedate Jet as advised by the dentist so that he could remove his wolf tooth. The vet and dentist turned up at almost the same time. The vet got to work immediately and sedated him. Whilst Jet was under sedation she also gave him his flu and tetanus jab. When she felt the sedation had taken effect she allowed the dentist to start his work. Within only a matter of minutes the dentist finished and gave me a tiny amount of crumbling tooth. I was amazed that Jet had apparently been in discomfort due to such a small tooth. I was also amazed at how this two-minute procedure had cost me best part of £150! The vet suggested that he stayed in his stable for at least a couple of hours in order for the sedation to wear off, but I decided to leave him in for the whole day. The last thing I wanted was to do was to put him out not fully alert and end up putting him in even more danger with the bullies in the field. After all, Jet was such a nice person. Every single time he had been set upon, he never once showed any signs of aggression. He would not even defend himself and had never so much as lifted a leg to any of the geldings. In a way I wish he had, that way he may have been respected more for it.

After two weeks there was no change and I was due to go back to work. I felt I had to say something to Cherie, the yard manager because there was no way I could go back to work, working twelve and a half hour shifts, knowing that Jet was still being treated like this. After discussing my concerns with Cherie, she had a chat with Greg and informed him of the situation. He understood completely and told me that I could move him indefinitely to a field solely for Jet. Again, this field was in the same location as the others but simply separated by wire. I was absolutely thrilled to bits that Jet could get out of the gelding field. As far as I could see he was going to have the best of both worlds now. He was going to be nearer to Dee and surrounded by horses nearby, but on his own so he could at last relax.

Monday 24th September – Jet gets his own residence

I turned Jet out immediately into his new paddock. He seemed very excited! He had a fast trot around the perimeter of his field and then he did what he enjoyed doing best, got stuck into the grass and actually seemed chilled out for the first time since being here. After ten minutes or so he threw himself on the floor and rolled and rolled. I was just so happy! Jet's new field was covered in poo from other horses so my mum and I spent nearly five full days clearing it. It was bloody hard work but worth it. The only downside to this field was that there was no running water in it, so I would have to carry buckets of water over into his field for him on a daily basis. This however, was such a small price to pay for hopefully having a happy horse at last.

Sunday 30th September 2007 –
Winter is upon us

I dreaded the winter months when the horses were stabled, especially as we were told when to bring our horses in. It was usually the last day in September that they had to start coming in at night. Although funnily enough I remember Amanda telling me not to stable Jet because he didn't like it, I remember thinking, 'Well, Jet will have to get used to it because horses are not allowed to winter out at our livery yard.' However, Jet had taken a real liking to his stable here and I found as long as he had loads of hay to occupy him he was absolutely fine. He was stabled next to Dee, which he was very happy about, but he also had Chunky on the other side of him, which he was less happy about. Chunky was quite a lot bigger than Jet and could therefore manage to get his head over the partition wall just to wind Jet up! Jet really hated this and often he would kick out at the stable wall out of pure frustration. One morning when I went to the stables I couldn't quite believe my eyes. Jet had obviously been pushed to his limits by Chunky and had practically kicked the dividing wall down between them. Luckily it was only plasterboard, which I knew, could be easily repaired but I was really worried that Jet may have injured himself in the process. Fortunately he was fine except for being quite agitated that day; perhaps he didn't get much sleep that night! I asked Mark if it would be possible for us to swap stables. That way, Jet could still be next to Dee but he would not have anyone next to him on his other side. He agreed to a swap around. I was so grateful. There is nothing worse knowing that your horse is unhappy but at least this is one situation we were able to resolve. That night we switched beds over and Jet seemed very happy with his new living arrangements. The plasterboards were soon replaced and at last we were all happy even though they were in. There is a certain amount of satisfaction to be had from leaving your horse all cosy and tucked up for the night when it is chucking it down with rain, blowing a gale and freezing cold.

Tuesday 13ᵗʰ November 2007-
Jet will make a fantastic driving horse?

As Jet had been advertised as a ride and drive, I thought it was about time that I seriously thought about driving Jet. Although he had been fairly good under saddle at this point, I thought at least the children could become more involved with him if we were able to drive him out together. I did however, only have limited driving experience which was a bit worrying. I owned a Shetland driving pony for a short while approximately twenty three years ago called Zelda. I was only about 15yrs old at the time. I acquired her through a friend of mine. This pony was due to become homeless as she was owned by an elderly couple who ran a pub who were soon to retire and move, and could therefore no longer look after her. I went along to see this pony and took pity on her due to her circumstances. I told the lady that I would go back to collect her later that week. She seemed like a real sweetie!

Within a week of having Zelda I noticed some strange behaviour patterns with her, so much so that I called the vet out. The vet wanted some background information on her but I had to tell him that all I really knew was that she came from a pub and belonged to an elderly couple. He said that she seemed to be withdrawing badly and asked me to contact her previous owners to see if they used to give her alcohol. It turned out that on a daily basis this poor pony was getting beer for breakfast dinner and tea and also had a few measures of shorts before bedtime. Just my luck, I owned an alcoholic pony! I knew I wasn't going to be able to afford her lifestyle. The vet said I would need to start giving her Guinness on a daily basis and reduce the amount very slowly.

During her withdrawal programme I did drive her to take her mind off things. I absolutely loved it! It took me a good few hours to fathom out the harness and how to put it on, but with a bit of support I got there in the end. She was very well behaved and also liked the work. The first time I ever took her out was quite an embarrassing event however. The yard that I kept her on was on the top of a steep hill. As we drove down it, her pace got quicker and quicker. At the time I wasn't sure what she was up to, but then I realised that at the bottom of the hill and just round the corner there was a pub. She had never seen it before, so she must have smelt it. We ended up trotting very fast down the hill and we finished up doing an emergency stop in the pub car park! She grounded herself and just refused to budge.

After just a few minutes we had a large audience who thought the whole situation was hilarious. I had to send someone in to buy her half a Guinness as she was adamant she wasn't moving anywhere! As soon as she had drunk her Guinness she was happy to go home. Needless to say a pony with a drink problem when I was only 15 yrs was too much for me. I simply could not afford her habit. I ended up giving her to a friend of mine in a nearby village where she carried out the rest of her days in her trap doing daily egg rounds. So, I did only have a few months driving experience, but I just loved it. I really thought Jet would make a fantastic driving horse and hoped that we could all enjoy Jet together now as a family.

The harness that I had ordered only a few days previously arrived and I excitedly looked through the bag of bits and bobs. I couldn't wait to take it to Jet to try it on him. I rushed out to our local saddlery and bought a Liverpool driving bit and attached it to his new bridle. The only thing we needed now was a little cart that he could pull. I decided that while I found one it would be a good idea to long rein him out with his harness and blinkers on to get him used to it again. He seemed very tetchy and panicky with the reins touching his side; I didn't think this was a great start. Due to this reaction I decided it was probably best to take him into the ménage for the first few times instead of walking him out on the roads. It became apparent that he hated his blinkers and with hindsight I can understand why really. Jet had always had a phobia of things approaching him unexpectedly from behind whether it be objects or noise. Wearing blinkers only exaggerated this problem.

Long reining in the ménage for the first few times was a little problematic! It wasn't a relaxed time for him at all. The whites of his eyes could be seen again and he was clearly unhappy with me being behind him with the reins touching him. It took several attempts in the school for him to accept the reins and my position, and when he finally looked more at ease I decided to take him for a short walk around the village. At first he seemed quite happy plodding around the roads which made me feel very keen to start driving him, however, I realised shortly after seeing cars on the road that this dream was never going to happen either. He was absolutely fine with any vehicles or bikes that came towards us, but anything that he heard coming from behind him terrified him. This was because he couldn't see what was making the noise as he had blinkers on. He would rapidly spin in the road so that he was then able to see what had been approaching him. Despite persevering on a number of occasions with him, I decided that I should no longer pursue this idea, as it would only have been a matter of time before someone got hurt. It was bad enough Jet spinning round in the road, but if he had tried to do that with a cart behind him it would have been an accident waiting to happen! I wasn't prepared to take that risk, especially with my children. Approximately six months later I reluctantly put the harness on Ebay to see if I could sell it. Similar items on there were going for nearly the price I paid for mine so I wasn't too worried about loosing much money on it.

Sunday 6th January 2008 –
Jet can only canter on his left leg

Emily and I rode Jet as often as we could during the winter months in the ménage. It was quite off-putting in there when it was dark. We had an old petrol generator that operated two dim lights and the noise it made was horrendous. The shadows that the lights created scared Jet sometimes. Despite this, we rode him at least three times a week in the school. It is true to say that Jet's best pace was his trot. When going forward in trot, he looked superb, with high leg carriage and stunning looks. His canter however, had much room for improvement! It was easy to tell he found it extremely awkward cantering in the ménage. It was quite heavy going, especially on a twenty meter circle. With much encouragement his canter did get better, but it didn't take us long to realise that he was hopeless at cantering on his right leg. We spent hours trying all sorts of things that would aid a correct strike-off, but he just found it so difficult. Even whilst lunging he would always strike off on his left leg. We decided that it was time to start having lessons with him in order to crack the cantering problem we clearly had.

Both Emily and I had had several lessons by this time, and it was fair to say that Jet's overall work in the ménage had improved. Our instructor Freddie was very patient with us and even had a go himself at trying to get Jet to canter on his right leg. I was glad when even he encountered a few problems with him as I thought it was just us! Eventually though, he did get him cantering around beautifully on his right leg. As it had taken him some time to achieve this, he suggested that we put a jump up so that we could trot up to it and hopefully, get a canter on the right leg straight after the jump. I was a little apprehensive about trying this idea, only because we hadn't conquered the cantering so I thought that perhaps jumping was a bit too advanced for him! Anyway, we decided that Freddie knew best and gave it a go. Jet absolutely loved the idea of popping over a small jump and he even got a little excited about it. more importantly though we got a canter on the right leg straight after the jump. As soon as I realised that he was on the correct leg I shouted with excitement, "Yippee!" The small audience that were present were laughing at our squeals of happiness, but to us it really was such an achievement. We continued to have fortnightly lessons with Jet and slowly but surely we found ourselves heading in the right direction with him.

Monday 14th April 2008 –
Jet is still having teething problems

Both Emily and I had noticed that Jet had started head shaking quite a lot whilst being ridden. As this was a new thing for him I decided to get the dentist back out to check him over just in case he was having further problems in his mouth. This time I used a more local dentist who was used by the others up at the yard. She came to visit him and had a quick look in his mouth. She knew immediately what the problem was. She said that the previous dentist had broken off his wolf tooth at the gum and left the entire root still in there. She went on to explain that the gum had since grown over that area and had become sore for him, especially when the bit rubbed against it. She said the root would need to come out and that the only way of doing this was to sedate him again and the vet would need to surgically cut the gum to enable the dentist to remove the root. I was very pleased that I had rung her as I felt terrible that he may have been in pain.

Thursday 17th April 2008 –
Remainder of wolf tooth to be removed

Yet again, the dentist and vet arrived. I was getting to know the vets quite well and was even on first name terms with some! Jet was sedated once more and I stayed with him to assist the dentist in supporting his head whilst she got to work on him. Being a nurse, there is not much that turns my stomach, but when the vet cut into his gum, there was just so much blood and because it was my boy, it did make me feel a bit queasy. The dentist had one hell of a job to remove the remainder of the root, but after almost an hour the job was done. Jet was almost asleep during the procedure and did not appear to be in any discomfort. As before, he had to spend the rest of the day in his stable whilst the sedation had time to wear off. It was a horrible wet rainy day so he didn't seem to mind this at all. The dentist was confident that she had removed it all and advised me to keep him off work for at least five days. I rode him after the said time and was absolutely amazed that the head shaking had ceased! He must have felt so much better. I was so happy.

Saturday 3rd May 2008 -
Vetting papers translated

The winning bidder of my harness was an experienced driving lady who knew lots about horses, and she was intrigued to know why I was selling it. When I had given her a brief explanation of how I had come to get Jet and how he had been sold as a ride and drive, she asked me if he came with any paperwork. I told her that he came with a French vetting certificate and that was about it really. She asked me what the vetting said about him. I had to be truthful with her and said that I didn't really know as my French was pretty rubbish! She told me that she had a friend who was fluent in French and that if I somehow got a copy of Jet's paperwork to her she would ask her friend to translate it for me. I was thrilled. I copied the documents and sent them to her straight away.

No more than a week later I received an email from this lady. It explained a lot. Firstly, when I had told her about the micro-chipping scenario she said that in France many horses are chipped in the top of their tails as opposed to their necks. This shocked me somewhat, as it meant that Jet now possibly had two micro-chips in him, one in his neck and the other in his tail!

'Oh well,' I thought, 'two had to be better than none!' Secondly, according to the translation of vetting papers, he was registered on the French horse database as a black pony of unknown pedigree born in 2001. In other words, he definitely was not a Friesian. His simple in hand vetting concluded that whilst he would lead and walk past obstacles with no problem and scored quite highly for this, his visual surprise was terrible and he only scored two out of five for this which meant that he was easily scared of things behind him (think we had found this out already!). It went on to say that although Jet had had a saddle on, he wasn't entirely relaxed about it, and that he didn't accept a rider easily. To summarise, it all indicated that he had the makings to be a nice horse but had only been lightly backed and was a bit on the nervous side. So basically, it was confirmation that he had been completely miss-sold to me as he had never done all the things that had been stated in his advert. The lady even went onto say that I should seek advice from the Citizens Advice Bureau with regards to sending him back and getting a full refund! Whilst I could see why some people would have returned him immediately and demanded their money back, I had firmly made up my mind he was going nowhere. Jet simply has the sweetest of natures and it was due to his super personality that I knew I would never part with him. Even if his issues became so bad that I became too scared to ride him, he would never be returned or sold because I loved him so much. He would simply become a pet.

Saturday 17th May 2008 –
Jet bolts with me!!

During a ride out with Mark on this beautiful morning Jet had been behaving impeccably, mind you he did always seem to be more relaxed hacking out with Dee. We had just decided to have a trot up a tractor track in a field when all of a sudden, for no apparent reason, Jet took off. Oh my god I was so scared! Jet was never the fastest of horses in fact you couldn't even class him as forward going, but believe me when he was in flight mode he could gallop extremely fast. So there we were galloping down this field and he was veering left through the crops. All I could see approaching us was a big concrete post in the ground that became closer and closer to us. I tried with all my might to yank him right to miss it and at this point I can remember shutting my eyes, hoping for the best. God only knows how, but we did manage to miss it. He came to an abrupt stop and both our hearts were beating so fast! I can remember thinking how lucky I was to have stayed on as I really thought we were going to part company. It wouldn't have been so bad if I could have told you what it was that scared Jet in the first place to warrant him bolting. The only thing that I could possibly think may have caused it was that ironically, for the first time that day I had worn a body protector. I wondered if it had hit the back of the saddle, or even his back, which may have set him off. Whatever the reason it was bloody scary, and I hoped that it would never happen again!

I was very fortunate that Dee had remained calm and stood still whilst we were flying through the field. If she had joined in with us I dread to think where we may have ended up! It was becoming more and more apparent that Jet appeared to have a phobia about large birds, especially pigeons and pheasants that flew out and surprised him. Each time this happened we were off at a rapid rate of knots and it didn't matter where we were. That was the really worrying thing about it. When I remembered back to my childhood, riding naughty ponies that used to tank off with me left right and centre, I never used to bat an eyelid. It was all part of the fun. Somehow now, being in my late thirties it just didn't have the same fun factor that it used to!

Monday 9th June 2008 –
Oh no, it's happened again!

It wasn't just me that Jet appeared to be bolting with when he was scared. He had done it with Emily to. She had been out on a ride with Jenna and as Jet had walked towards a gap in the hedge a lady came past on her bike. With no word of warning he galloped flat out in the opposite direction of the bike, in a blind panic. This was Emily's first experience of Jet and his flight mode and it really unnerved her, like it would have done to anyone. When she eventually managed to stop she jumped off him and walked him back home whilst she was getting over the shock of her bolting experience! The bolting was now becoming a real problem as it seemed to be getting more and more frequent. I recommended that Emily took him in the ménage more often at that point until we got the bolting under control. She agreed that it was the right decision for the short term.

Poor Jet was getting a very bad reputation on the yard, and people never seemed to have a good word to say about him. It also materialised that people thought I should just cut my losses and get rid of him. I felt very sorry for him as it was never a naughty bolt just because he wanted to; we always knew it was because he was completely panic stricken. Mind you, at least a naughty bolt can often be cured. I knew that we had our work cut out with him. Soon after this episode I had his back checked by a horsey chiropractor and all was fine. I just wanted to be sure that it was nothing physical that had caused this behaviour. He was pronounced fit and well, which was more than could be said for our nerves!

Friday 18th July 2008 –
Oh my god, it's like his twin brother!

I had just got in from town when Mark sent me a text message telling me that I should look at my emails. I threw my bags down and switched my computer on. I made myself a coffee in the time that it took to start up, and sat in my little office with intrigue as to what I was meant to be looking at. When I opened up the email from him, there was an attachment. The sub heading of the email was. 'What do you think?' I rapidly opened up the attachment and was absolutely gob-smacked at what I saw. It was a photo of a horse that looked identical to Jet. The breed of horse was a French Meren's horse, otherwise known as the Black Prince of the Pyrenees. I had never heard of this breed before. I excitedly googled 'Meren's horse' to find out more about them. I discovered that this breed are known for being docile and gentle. They stand between 14.2hh and 15.2hh, and they were traditionally raised in herds native to the Ariege Pyrenees. They are sure footed, noble and intelligent. They are naturally close to humans and therefore make the best of companions, and are only ever pure black. It also went on to say that like most ponies, the Merens have strong characters and that one must be firm to make them work.

I was completely astonished. Everything I read described Jet perfectly!   Although it was never been confirmed, I was now sure that Jet had little or no Friesian in him at all and would say that he was mostly a French Merens Horse. I was chuffed to bits, and the more research I did, the more positive I was that he was a Meren's after all.

I had been out for several non-eventful rides over the last few weeks and I wasn't sure whether it was just coincidental that we hadn't had many birds fly out at us, or if it was a case of Jet perhaps just growing out of it. We had had some really fun rides. I found that I still remained quite tense when hacking out, in anticipation of the bolting but the more and more I rode out and the less and less it happened, the better I felt about it. On this particular day I had been riding out with a Jenna. I was leading the way on Jet. We had been walking down a bridle way that was situated next to a wheat field. It was a scorching hot day and we were having a fantastic time, chatting about all sorts and catching up with gossip, when all of a sudden a pigeon flew out at Jet and I. Jet turned on a sixpence and galloped flat out through the wheat. The worst thing about this occasion was that not only had the pigeon flown out and scared him, it was actually chasing us across the field! As we got approximately half way across the field, the pigeon diverted and Jet suddenly stopped. No sooner than he had planted himself in the crop, a pheasant flew up out of the wheat and he tanked off yet again, this time in the opposite direction!

I'm not one for shouting and screaming when travelling uncontrollably on horse back, I usually tend to stay calm and put all my effort into stopping, but on this second occasion we were heading flat out towards an eight foot hedge! I screamed very loudly and even took my feet out of my stirrups in anticipation of a tactical dismount. Luck must have been on my side that day, as unknown to me there was a very slight gap in the hedge. Jet managed to squeeze us both through and came to an abrupt stop on the other side of the hedge. I don't know who was shaken up more, me or him! All of a sudden, he must have realised that he had left Dee way behind. He stood there calling for her. I could feel his heart beating against my leg ten to the dozen (mind you I think mine was probably going even faster!).

I heard Jenna shout "Are you ok?"

I replied that I was ok, but I knew that it had really shaken me up big time. I felt that I had aged ten years during the past twelve months! I felt like crying on the way home and I was full of mixed emotions about Jet. I had got to the stage where it really scared me to ride him out, yet I knew the only way of desensitising him to birds and bikes was getting him out there in the thick of things, facing his fears head on. On the way home Jenna and I had a bit of a laugh about it, but it shouldn't really have been a laughing matter. I think I must still have been in a state of shock. Well, at least I hadn't fallen off!

Saturday 6th September 2008 – Burghley Cross Country Day!

I had still been thinking very hard about what was best to do with Jet and had finally come to the decision that I just needed to get on with it and try and stop worrying about the 'what if's'.

I was very excited as me and a couple of friends were heading off to Burghley for the day to watch the cross-country. We had arranged to meet other friends from the stables there and were sure that we were all in for a treat that day. We had a pleasant journey and it must have taken us approximately one hour and twenty minutes to get there. After some searching we managed to meet up with our other friends. It was nearly lunch time at this point and we had a very civilised lunch together followed by a few bottles of wine. It was great! The cross-country started and we slowly made our way round the course to watch riders at most of the jumps. This in itself was extremely comical as a lot of the course was thick with mud as there had been heavy rainfall for days. People were slipping over left right and centre! By the end of the day we were all worn out and spent out. I had bought Jet loads of gizmos and gadgets, and watching the jumping had given me the jumping bug. I couldn't wait to get home to pop Jet over a few fences (nothing like those at Burghley though!).

Knowing that he had never been to show I had often wondered how he would react at one, although the prospect did concern me as when Jet had come across other horses that he didn't know while out hacking, he often went berserk! I thought that the idea of going to a show might completely blow his mind. Never mind, I could live in hope.

Friday 26ᵗʰ December 2008 –
The pain was too intense

Early Boxing Day morning I had arranged to meet my friend Danielle for a ride round our local woods as the weather forecast had been good. We were in good spirits and enjoying the cold, crisp, dry morning. Danielle and I were busy chatting about who had received the naffest present for Christmas and generally having a laugh while we trotted through the woods. In the distance I could see that we were fast approaching a boggy section which covered almost the entire track. Whilst Jet has feet the size of dinner plates, and is generally very sure footed, he very much dislikes thick mud. Thinking I was doing him a favour by avoiding it, I kept him on a tight rein and asked him to tiptoe as far over to the left as possible. For some bizarre reason, I leant forward and looked down his right shoulder to see if we were out of the mud, at which point Jet happily continued trotting, managing to take me straight in to a tree. My left knee was wedged in the branches, and as this was slightly alien for Jet, he did what he did best, panicked and ran! I felt my left leg get dragged so far behind it almost felt as though it was going on the top of his back! A dozen or so canter strides later I managed to stop him.

This was one of Danielle's first hacks out on her lovely cob Murphy. She hadn't owned him for very long and she was also a novice rider. Of course Murphy also took off with Jet! This was her first canter experience out on a hack. She said though that in a strange way she said she had enjoyed it, despite the fact that neither of us had got control of our horses! Tears were rolling down my face. I had never felt pain like it (well maybe childbirth was slightly worse, but only very slightly worse). When I got back home that morning, the first thing I did was remove my jodhpurs so I could see what damage I had done. The entire knee from back to front was bright purple! I had also managed to put several holes in my jods and where these had been I had some deep and nasty cuts too. The bruising took approximately six weeks to go down but despite the pain, only a few days later I was back in the saddle. What a glutton for punishment I am!

Sunday 22nd February 2009 –
Our first long ride out on our own

Although Jet had been quite brave riding out on his own on the odd occasion, I decided it was about time I ventured a little further with him. It was a cool calm day and I hoped that as it was a Sunday there wouldn't be much in the way of traffic about on the roads. I headed up to the yard early. No one was around at the time of leaving the yard so I left a note on the tack room board stating what time I had left and where I was going, just in case anything untoward happened. We had been out for about an hour and in that time we had done lots of trotting and had had a lovely steady canter on a stubble field.

As we neared home, just walking on the road, I could hear some traffic approaching us from behind. I could feel Jet tense so I just kept my leg on him and talked to him. A 4x4 came past very considerately, followed by a camper van that looked and sounded like it should have been at the scrap yard! It made so much noise that Jet bolted again. For the first time ever though, it was on the road. A guy on a mountain bike had being following the camper van and we found ourselves galloping flat out towards the cyclist. I was shouting, "Stop! Get out of the way!" at the top of my voice as Jet was getting closer and closer, but I soon realised that the bloke was listening to his music and was totally oblivious to what was going on behind him (which was probably just as well!). I managed to bring Jet back to a walk just as I got level with the guy on his bike. He turned his head and looked at us with a very shocked expression on his face as we were going side by side next to each other! I just could not wait to get home. Perhaps this 'riding out on your own' business isn't all its cracked up to be after all!

Literally just a few hundred feet from home, Greg came round the corner on his quad bike. Luckily he slowed right down and asked me what Jet was like with quad bikes. I replied that I didn't know but in view of recent activities he probably wouldn't like them! He stopped and we chatted for a few moments. After our chat he waited for us to walk past him and then gave his bike a bit of throttle as he had stopped on a slope. Well, I'm sure Jet thought he had been shot at once again! We ended up galloping the remainder of the ride home and eventually skidded to a halt in the yard. I was so pleased to get back in one piece. My legs were so like jelly when I dismounted that I nearly fell over! I untacked Jet and poured a very strong coffee. I can remember thinking, 'I'm getting way too old for all this!'

Saturday 2nd May 2009 – I wonder if????

I sat watching Danielle having a lesson on Murphy and he was going really well. After about thirty minutes into their lesson I noticed that he started to tire and he began to throw his head up constantly. After several minutes, Freddie suggested that Danielle alter her running martingale to a standing martingale, to avoid her getting a broken nose! As if by miracle, as soon as it was altered, Murphy was as good as gold and the head tossing stopped. This got me thinking about Jet. There was a pattern in Jets bolting. As soon as he had been scared by something he would throw his head up really high and then proceed to gallop. It was almost as though he needed to get his head up that high in order to initiate the momentum of his gallop. This made me think. I wondered if putting a standing martingale on him would have the same effect and maybe even stop him from bolting.

Tuesday 19th May 2009 –
I don't want to speak to soon......

I seem to have a reformed horse. I have had several rides out on Jet since putting him in a standing martingale he appears to be a changed person. I rode him out today just around the block as I was running short of time. I went out with another friend and we were having a trot down a bridleway when a pigeon flew out at us. I could feel Jet tense and he did manage to run forward maybe two or three strides but because he was physically unable to throw his head up high. We didn't go anywhere! In fact I think because he had tried to throw his head up, it had obviously put a sudden pressure on his nose from his noseband and he really didn't like it, so he quickly stopped in his tracks and I made a real fuss of him. I just knew from how close the pigeon had been, that under normal circumstances we would certainly have been off! I was utterly amazed, thrilled and even excited. Have we at long last conquered the bolting problem?

Saturday 27ᵗʰ June 2009 –
Get painting that lorry

One of the girls at the stables called Kath was due to put her horse lorry in for its MOT and asked if anyone would like to help her give it a makeover with a lick of paint. She also offered to give a free ride out to anyone that helped. This sounded very appealing, as apart from moving Jet's home I had never actually taken him anywhere. During this weekend quite a few of us rallied round and got the best part of the paintwork finished. The weather was hot and most of us managed to get sunburnt whilst we had been up ladders wielding paintbrushes, but it was all good fun! The hours just seemed to fly by as we painted away quite happily. Kath went to our local supermarket and bought lunch back for everyone. It was really lovely and a nice chance for us all to get together for a good old gossip and chat. It looked like a completely different lorry by the time we had finished it. We had all done a good job. Within a fortnight Kath's lorry had successfully passed its MOT. We were all over the moon and were sure that our painting team had been a contribution to it passing its test!

Just as I had left the yard for the night my mobile rang. It was Kath. She told me of a show that she had heard about that was taking place the following weekend, and as it was due to be a quiet affair and close to home she asked if I wanted to take Jet. All of a sudden I felt a rush of butterflies in my stomach. A show? Me and Jet? I told her I would have to think about it as I was unsure of my shifts for that next week. The truth is, she had taken me by complete surprise and I really thought Jet wouldn't be up to going to a show as he had never been to one before! As it was, on rides out if he met up with unfamiliar horses, he threw wobblers. What on earth would he be like surrounded by strange horses and events?! I spoke to Emily about it and between us we decided that as it was a small show it would be good experience for him to go and have a look, even if the worst case scenario happened and we had to load him straight back up and take him home again due to highly strung behaviour. The more I thought about it, the bigger the butterflies got!

Sunday 2nd August 2009 –
Show day

I arrived at the stables at 6.30am in order to get Jet prepared for the show. As sod's law would dictate, Jet had to be the filthiest horse in the field! I could have cried when I saw him. I bought him into the yard and really didn't know where to start first. I decided that starting at the bottom and working up would be a good plan, so I set to scrubbing his feet and hosing his legs down. We were due to be picked up in approximately 2 hours so I didn't have long. Luckily Emily and Jenna got to the yard early and we all mucked in together to make him look absolutely gorgeous. It took us almost an hour to put his long mane into a lattice plait, but we were so glad we did as he really looked the part if nothing else! Before we knew it the lorry had arrived. Jet was all booted and suited for the occasion and we were all hoping that he would just remain calm.

The laugh of it all was that the show that we were taking him to was none other than a local show jumping event. We had only popped him over the odd fence or two at home, so even if he behaved like the perfect gentleman there wasn't much we were going to be able to do anyway! Remaining positive, we walked him over to the lorry and he went straight in like a sweetheart. This surprised me as the lorry engine was still running at the time, yet he didn't seem bothered by this at all. Emily and I travelled in the cab of the lorry. Jet appeared to have stayed calm and relaxed throughout the journey and there were hardly any movement sounds coming from him at all. Ten minutes later we arrived at the show, followed by Jenna in her car. The ramp came down and out he came. He took his time coming off the ramp and during this time he had a good look around to see where he was and what was going on.

Fortunately we were one of the first to arrive so there wasn't much going on at all. When he was finally out, we took his boots, rug and bandages off and gave him yet another groom. He was so shiny and, being Jet black, he looked stunning. We decided to walk him around the grounds to get a feel for the place. After a good few minutes I realised that he was actually fine and he didn't seem phased by anything, so I handed him to Jenna and asked her to hold him whilst Emily and I could look at some of the jumps, not that we had any intention of jumping them! Jenna had previously been busy videoing Jet whilst being loaded and unloaded from the lorry but unfortunately at this point the camera had stopped rolling, and it was such a shame. Just as we had walked off we heard this loud shriek of "JET!" As we turned, we saw Jet lying on the floor. He had made himself at home and had decided that it was a good time for a roll in the mud. Emily and I went running over to him and managed to get him up, but not before he had covered one side of himself in mud – the little bugger!

We quickly took him back over to the horse lorry where we got the grooming box out and yet again tried to clean him up! All his white plaiting bands had now turned brown and he had a few wet patches of mud over him, but it wasn't long before he looked amazing again.

I got him tacked up and I quickly changed into some clean jods. I got on him, still feeling slightly apprehensive. It was a really windy day and I thought that this would have added to our problems. I rode him round in the paddock where the horse lorries were parked, and just did a bit of walk and trot with him. He seemed quite on edge and for this reason I felt that if I took him over to the other horses this may get worse. Kath said she thought I would be better off getting him over with the others and taking it from there. I agreed that I should try it just to see if he would settle. As soon as we arrived in the fields where it was all happening, Jet seemed as laid back as he is at home! We were all totally thrilled at how calm he appeared. Even Emily said that she was prepared to get on and ride him about for a while as he seemed so relaxed. He had also caught a few people's eye and we had strangers approach us saying how great he looked and asking what breed he was. I felt like a very proud mummy!

I rode him to the warm up area. We trotted and even had a small canter. He was just so good. There was a very small practice jump that had been put up and I found myself happily sailing over that too! I couldn't believe what was going on. We had all ended up at this jumping event with Jet. Deep down I really had thought that I wouldn't even be able to get on him and here we were cantering over practice jumps! I was so pleased with him. Kath then approached me and suggested that we try jumping the clear round. I thought, 'Why not!' There were only four jumps out in a large ménage, each of which had to be jumped twice. They were very small but fine for us. I excitedly took Jet in and it was just like riding him at home. He was hard work to keep going forward at times, but I could tell he was having a ball. We came out having completed a clear round and I felt like shrieking with joy at the top of my voice! I was then given our very first rosette. I was so happy, especially as

Tom and our boys had just arrived in time to see us in action. I truly never thought I would see the day when Jet and I would be at a show together with Jet actually jumping and enjoying himself so much. It was quite an emotional moment!

When Jet had had a few minutes rest Emily took him into the clear round jumping. Sadly they knocked one down so didn't get a clear round. I think all of the excitement of the day had worn him out! After watching some of the others jumping in the main arena we took Jet back to the lorry and got him prepared for his short journey home. When he was ready I walked him towards the ramp of the lorry. He stood there with his two front feet on it, looking around the field, almost as if to say, 'Actually I would rather stay for a bit longer as I have had so much fun.' I showed him a carrot and he soon went in. What a funny character he is. I'm sure that there are people down at our yard that think I am completely barmy but I just can't help it, I love my Jet so much!! When we arrived back at the yard, the ramp came down and Jet looked straight out to see where he was. He seemed happy to be home, as we all were after such a fun morning out. Roll on our next show!

Monday 24th August 2009 – Final entry

I had decided that the show was going to be the last entry in my diary, whether it had proven to be good or bad. The fact that we finished on a high is certainly the best way to finish anything in life. Jet is still far from the horse that was advertised, but I firmly believe given another year or so and he may well be (all except for the driving that its!). Oh, and the height thing, he will never be 15.2hh either. He now stands just under 15hh, and as he is approximately eight years old so I don't expect he will get any bigger!

To date he still has problems cantering on his right leg in the ménage but we are still working on it and getting there slowly. He is enjoying the few small fences that we have put up for him and as long as the course is on the left rein he is absolutely fine! He still gets twitchy if large birds flap at him, although he certainly seems to be getting better. Next year I have decided I would like to try some cross-country with him if I can pluck up enough courage, as I believe he may be good at this. Both Emily and I have been enjoying hacking Jet for some time now. We take him out in company of other horses mainly, but also on his own occasionally just to try and build on his confidence. When hacking out with other horses he feels he has to be in front and if he's not, somehow he will find a way of getting there. For a little person he has such a huge character, he really makes us laugh. He still adores Dee and every time he sees her he gives her an excited whinny. Unfortunately the feeling isn't mutual, as Dee really isn't bothered by Jet at all.

My eldest son who is now aged eleven years, and who has had no previous riding experience has just started to ride Jet, walking him in the ménage or walking him on a lead rein around the village. He is thrilled to be doing so, and Jet has been such a good boy for him. After much love and perseverance he seems to be becoming our **** true family horse. *****

When I think back to the time that people were suggesting that I cut my losses and get rid of him, I am just so pleased that I didn't listen. If he had gone back, he could have ended up in a horrible home or much worse, maybe ending up going for meat. I believe that we have a special relationship/friendship, and know that he trusts me implicitly. I will never let him down. If there is a small message to be passed on out there, it would be not to be quite as naïve as I was when it came to purchasing a horse on the Internet. But hey, I really can't knock it. I love my boy and he is one of the best things that have ever happened to me!!!! I do hope that you have enjoyed reading about our journey over the last couple of years and I am sure we will have many more exciting adventures in the future. You never know, in a few years to come there could be a sequel if the sagas continue.